Waltraud Kokot (ed.)

# Beyond the White Tower – Transformations in Thessaloniki

# lines

Beiträge zur Stadtforschung
aus dem Institut für Ethnologie
der Universität Hamburg

herausgegeben von

Waltraud Kokot

Band 4

LIT

# Beyond the White Tower – Transformations in Thessaloniki

## Ethnographic case studies on local aspects of urban change

edited by

Waltraud Kokot

LIT

∞

Gedruckt auf alterungsbeständigem Werkdruckpapier entsprechend
ANSI Z3948 DIN ISO 9706

Titelfoto: Kasper de Jong

**Bibliographic information published by the Deutsche Nationalbibliothek**
The Deutsche Nationalbibliothek lists this publication in the Deutsche Nationalbibliografie; detailed bibliographic data are available in the Internet at http://dnb.d-nb.de.

ISBN 978-3-8258-0917-1

**A catalogue record for this book is available from the British Library**



Auslieferung/Verlagskontakt:
Fresnostr. 2 48159 Münster
Tel. +49 (0)251–62 03 20 Fax +49 (0)251–23 19 72
e-Mail: lit@lit-verlag.de http://www.lit-verlag.de

Distributed in the UK by: Global Book Marketing, 99B Wallis Rd, London, E9 5LN
Phone: +44 (0) 20 8533 5800 – Fax: +44 (0) 1600 775 663
http://www.centralbooks.co.uk/acatalog/search.html

Distributed in North America by:

Transaction Publishers
New Brunswick (U.S.A.) and London (U.K.)

Transaction Publishers
Rutgers University
35 Berrue Circle
Piscataway, NJ 08854

Phone: +1 (732) 445 - 2280
Fax: + 1 (732) 445 - 3138
for orders (U. S. only):
toll free (888) 999 - 6778
e-mail:
orders@transactionspub.com

# Beyond the White Tower: transformations in Thessaloniki.

## Ethnographic case studies on local aspects of urban change.


Herausgegeben von:
Waltraud Kokot

Head of Project:
Waltraud Kokot

Researchers:
Sarah Brammann I Elke Haas I Berit Langeneck
Kathrin Leven I Nikola Spilok-Malanda


EUROPEAN PORT CITIES

## City of Thessaloniki, Research Areas

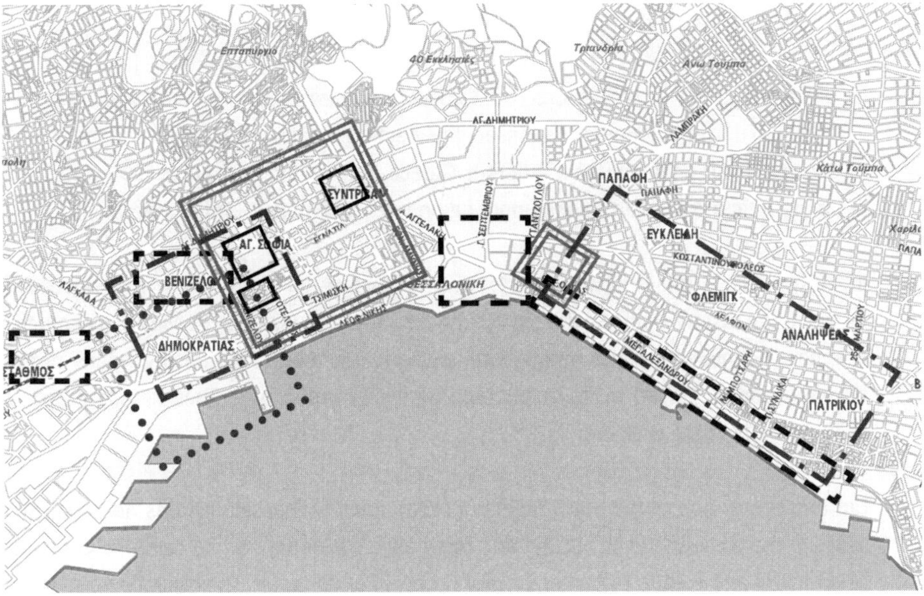


Research Area: Albanians (dotted line)

Research Area: Russian vendors (solid line)

Research Area: Africans (double line)

Research Area: Homelessness (dashed line)

Research Area: Jews (dash-dot line)

# Introduction: transformations in Thessaloniki

Waltraud Kokot

> "The first time I visited Salonica ... I knew I had been transported into another world...From the moment I crossed the hectic confusion of Vardar square ... I sensed the presence of a different Greece, less in thrall to an ancient past, more intimately linked to neighbouring peoples, languages, and cultures."

In these words, Mark Mazower (2004:1) sets the stage for his review of Thessaloniki´s multicultural history. Entering the city for the first time, the historian senses five centuries of ethnic heterogeneity and intercultural exchange in the few remaining traces of the Ottoman period. Linked to its neighbours by the Ottoman past, Thessaloniki presents itself as a city of the Balkans.

But this is only one of the many facets of urban identity Thessaloniki has adapted until today. In the present, the city is first and foremost a major port, and a centre of commerce, industry and culture in contemporary Greece. For centuries, Thessaloniki was known as "*La Madre de Israel*" (Jewish Museum of Thessaloniki 2007). Referring to the dramatic and violent exchange of populations following the Asia Minor Campaign in 1922, Thessaloniki became known as the Greek "Capital of Refugees" (Ioannou 1984). In 1997, Thessaloniki was elected "Cultural Capital of Europe", initiating a thorough renovation of major parts of the city centre, as well as belated references to the city´s alleged multicultural heritage (Agelopoulos 2000). Lately, due to its central position in a politically and economically transforming South Eastern Europe, Thessaloniki has staked its (not uncontested) claims as the new "Capital of the Balkans".

The following articles deal with small-scale effects of social, political, economic and demographic transformations in Thessaloniki since the end of the 1980s, which have also affected the city´s changing image and public presentation. The presence of new immigrants, mainly from Albania and the former Soviet Union, but also from Asia and Africa has become quite visible in Thessaloniki´s public space. Less obvious, but equally related to the transformations of the past two decades, is the increase of homeless persons spending their days and nights in the inner city and along the waterfront (*paralía*).

Beginning gentrification: partially restored structures in the commercial district (Photo: Kasper de Jong)

The last years have also brought significant changes in the city´s urban image and public presentation. After decades of neglect and the loss of many architectural treasures, at least some of the *art nouveau* buildings in the commercial centre, which was completely rebuilt after the Great Fire of 1917, have been saved and restored. The much older *Ladadika* area close to the port, once the seat of wholesalers of oil and grain, had fallen into disrepair and turned into a ramshackle red light quarter since the 1950s. Condemned to be torn down, it was saved virtually in the last minute (Mavromatis 1996) and has been turned into an expensive, but well-frequented entertainment area. Its restored structures now give at least an impression of Thessaloniki´s inner city before the twentieth century. In line with this renewed interest in Thessaloniki´s architectural heritage in the context of the Cultural Capital events, is a changed representation of the city´s multicultural history. Until the 1980s, Thessaloniki was exclusively presented as a Byzantine / Greek city. References to the Jewish community were scarce, and the Ottoman past was virtually absent from tourist guides or other presentations by the municipality. Recently, also Ottoman buildings remaining in the Upper City (Ano Polis) have been restored, and the multicultural past is now presented as a focal point of the city´s identity (Kyrtsis 2000:11). In this context, the opening of the Jewish Museum in 1997 is of particular significance, demonstrating a new assertiveness of diaspora identity in Thessaloniki.

## Thessaloniki in historical context [1]

Around the year 315 B.C. the Macedonian king Kassandros combined the city of Therma with twenty-five other communities and founded the city of Thessaloniki, which he named after his wife, a sister of Alexander the Great` s. The importance of the city extended beyond the immediate region already in Antiquity. In the year 146 B.C. it became the capital of the roman province of Macedonia. In the 6th century, Thessaloniki was a subcentre of the Byzantine Empire, second to Constantinople.

The invasion of Thessaloniki by the Sarassins in the year 904 marks the beginning of a series of sieges, conquests and destructions. Thessaloniki was ruled successively by Normans, Venitians and Ottomans before reverting temporarily back to Byzance, and in 1430 – the city was by then considerably depopulated – was taken by Murad II for the Ottoman Empire. In the year 1453, Constantinople was conquered by the Ottomans. The entire area of what is now Greece became, with the exception of the Ionic islands, a part of the Ottoman Empire.

A feudal state composed of many cultures, the Ottoman Empire was organized along military principles. The Ottomans made up the elite, mostly possessing large estates and political and military posts. The colonized peoples were farmers, artisans and merchants; as non-muslims they had no access to military or administrative positions. The Jews and Christians, as "people of the book", were not supposed to be forcibly converted to Islam[2]. They had to submit special taxes, but were for the most part entitled to administrate their own affairs. The administration of their communities (*millet*), along with responsibility for the taxes, was in the hands of the religious leaders. In the case of the Greek-orthodox population, designated as *rum*-millet, this was the Patriarchy of Constantinople.

[1] The following summary is primarily based on publications on the history of Thessaloniki by Enepekidis (1982, 1988), Vakalopoulos (1983) and Papagiannopoulos (1982). Clogg (1979), Hering, Demetriou, Kelpanidis (1983), Mazower (2004), Richter (1973, 1988, 1990) and Vakalopoulos (1985) served as primary sources for the history of Greece.

[2] Although throughout the course of history forced conversions appeared repeatedly.

In the year 1492, the edict of Alhambra led to the eviction of the Jews from all the Spanish holdings. About 20 000 Sephardic Jews, who had been accepted into the Ottoman Empire, were established in the practically depopulated city of Thessaloniki. Through their contacts with Spain, Italy and the Netherlands, Thessaloniki developed again into the main commercial centre of the Balkan region. Jews, Greeks, Turks, Armenians, Slavs and Roma formed the ethnic mosaic of the city, with the Jews representing the majority of the population (Mazower 2004; Molho 1981; Moutzopoulos 1980:24-25; Lewkowicz 1990a and 2006). *Ladino*, a form of Castilian written with Hebrew letters, was a major language in Thessaloniki up until the destruction of the Jewish community in the Second World War.

Around the beginning of the 19th century, nationalistic movements developed in the border regions of the Ottoman Empire. The Greek fight for independence began in 1821. Although at this time the Ottoman Empire was already economically and politically weak and largely dependent on Russia and Europe, the tide turned in Greece's favour only after the involvement of Britain and Russia. Greece became independent in 1830. Britain and Russia decided on a monarchy for the country's form of government. In 1833, the Bavarian prince Otto was nominated as the first king of Greece. The country at that time consisted only of southern and central Greece. Further regions, such as Crete, were added in the course of the 19th century.

The Ottoman Empire of the end of the 19th century was characterized by attempts at internal reform, an increasing economic and political dependence on the West, and the development of Young Turkish nationalism, which increasingly influenced the government in Istanbul (Peters 1961:127 ff; Pack 1991:13). The first of the Balkan Wars broke out in 1912, the second in 1913. The Ottoman Empire lost large parts of its domain, Greece won the regions of Epiros, Macedonia, Crete and West Thracia. In October 1912, the Greek army entered Thessaloniki. In 1913, under the Treaty of Bucarest, Thessaloniki officially became a part of the Greek state.

Since the beginning of the 19th century, the Ottoman Empire had, under the influence of the Young Turk movement, reverted to a policy of assimilation of ethnic and national minorities, which turned into prosecution and extermination in the Armenian genocide of

1915. Armenians from Turkey found refuge in the Armenian community of Thessaloniki, although a majority of the refugees moved on to other diaspora communities in France and the United States (Abels 1991; Gust 1991; Walker 1991; Schwalgin 2004).

The history of Greece at the beginning of the twentieth century is characterized by a series of economic and political crises. In World War I, Greece remained neutral at first, but it finally joined in the war against Germany after the occupation of Thessaloniki by French and English troupes. In 1917, a great fire devastated large parts of the city. The old city centre was almost completely destroyed, leaving more than 50 000 people homeless.

After the war, a division of Turkey was effected in the Treaty of Sèvres. Greece secured the Greek-populated territories in Asia Minor: this included areas around Constantinople (Istanbul), Smyrna (Izmir), in Pontos (on the Black See coast) and in Anatolia. When in May 1919, the Greek army marched into Smyrna (Izmir), they were acclaimed as saviours by the Greek population there, but raids against the Turkish population resulted in a strengthening of laws against the Greek minority. Turkish troupes destroyed Greek settlements in the Pontos (Black Sea) area. The nationalists under Mustafa Kemal did not recognize the Treaty of Sèvres and took action against the government in Istanbul.

In 1921, the Greek advance was stopped, and after the great powers retracted their support of Greece, and in 1922, the Greek army was defeated. The Greek quarter in Smyrna was destroyed and a large part of the population was killed. Thousands of people died while fleeing or as a result of deportations. The defeated Greek soldiers fled with the Greek civilian population to the west coast. These defeats and the subsequent suffering of the Greek population have entered Greek history as the "catastrophe of Asia Minor" (*mikrasiatiki katastrophi*). The memory of flight and persecution have long influenced the relationship of the Greek public to that "hostile neighbour", Turkey. A population exchange between Greece and Turkey was agreed to in 1923, in which the religion in first place, the language in second would be the deciding factor on who was treated as "greek" or as "turkish". About 50 000 Muslims, mostly from the North, were forced to leave Greece. Greece, with a population of about 4.5 million, had to take in 1.5 million refugees from Asia Minor. Thessaloniki became – along with Athens and the Piraeus – a main destination for the flow of refugees. Practically the whole Muslim population of about 20 000 had left the city. Over 100 000 refugees were settled in Thessaloniki. New settlements evolved on the city's edges, the population rose to 220 000 (Papaioannou, Traganou 1974:37; Papadopoulou-Symeonidou 1975:17).

After a series of government crises, General Metaxas established in 1936, with the king's authorization, a military dictatorship. The plan was for an evolution into a fascist state, taking Italy and Germany as a model, but a large fascist popular movement never managed to take hold in Greece. In 1940, Italy's attempt to occupy Greece failed; however, in April 1941, the Germans occupied the country. In the Second World War, over 100 000 people died in Greece. Practically the whole Jewish population emigrated or was murdered. In Thessaloniki alone, 43 000 people were deported to the death camps.

After short-lived attempts at democracy at the beginning of the sixties, and a military dictatorship since 1967, parliamentary democracy was reintroduced in 1974. In a referendum, the majority decided against a reintroduction of the monarchy. Since 1987, Greece is a full member of the European Union. In 1997, Thessaloniki was nominated Cultural Capital of Europe.

## Thessaloniki as site of ethnographic research

Thirty years ago, in his overview of the state of research in Mediterranean anthropology, John Davis (1977:10) called for a much-needed ethnography of Thessaloniki. Although in the meantime, urban studies have developed into a well-established sub-field of anthropology, the number of urban ethnographies in Greece is still limited. The monograph on Thessaloniki, called for by Davis, is still missing today. Needless to say, the following articles do not pretend to fill this gap either.

Although estimated 60% of Greece´s population are by now living in cities (Europa auf einen Blick 2007), urban anthropological research in Greece has been (and still is) quite rare. With few exceptions, current research interests seem to concentrate predominantly on questions of the symbolic construction of identities, gender, and discourse, studied mostly on a village level.

As Vermeulen pointed out in his summary review of 1983, anthropological studies in Greece have long been dominated by paradigms explicitly precluding urban research. In the course of Greece´s nation-building process, the founding generation of Greek *laographia* (folklore studies) saw their task not only in documenting rural cultural traditions, but in (re)creating a Greek national folklore (Kyriakidou-Nestoros 1978; Herzfeld 1982). In turn, Western anthropologists were severely limited by a dominating concept of Mediterranean "peasant" societies, dating back to the pioneering studies by Friedl (1962) and Campbell (1964). Nonetheless, the rapid rate of urbanization in Greece after WW II could not remain unnoticed. In the 1970s, some anthropologists began to follow the villagers to the big cities, but the village still remained in focus, drawing major attention to rural-urban links (Gutenschwager 1971; Kenna 1976; Vermeulen 1970). Since the 1980es, only a small number of monographs has supplemented Vermleulen´s list. In his study of Rethymnon, Herzfeld (1991) investigates the traces of history in the public memory and physical urban space. Hirschon (1989) provides an ethnography of a refugee quarter in Athens settled by Asia Minor refugees.

While the history of Thessaloniki has been documented in a host of publications, only few ethnographic studies on Thessaloniki have been published. Lewkowicz´s monograph (2006) on the history, memory and identity formation of the Jewish Community, and Schwalgin´s (2004) study on the Armenian communities of Athens and Thessaloniki are notable exceptions, but both studies focus on selected diaspora communities rather than on Thessaloniki as such. Kokot's (1996) study on the former refugee quarter Kato Toumba has remained unpublished, as well as Stroux' (2006) recent research on street vending as a livelihood strategy among refugees in Thessaloniki. Ourania Rapti´s study on dockworkers and gentrification in the *Ladadika* area is currently still in process (although documented in a short paper in 2006).

## Key concepts and points of departure

Also the following articles cannot claim to present a comprehensive ethnographic view of Thessaloniki. As they are based on student research projects with a very limited time frame, their scope is necessarily limited to small-scale observations and in-depth interviews with a limited number of informants. Nonetheless, as case-studies, they attempt to investigate and demonstrate some local effects of the rapid economic and political transformations Thessaloniki has been experiencing as a port and frontier city.

The practice of ethnographic fieldwork is a core element of the course of studies at the institute of anthropology (Institut für Ethnologie) at Hamburg university. Before finishing their studies, all students majoring in anthropology are required to design and pursue a field project of five to six weeks duration, which requires at least one semester for preparation and for data analysis. While most students pursue these projects on their own or in small independent groups, guided field excursions are offered biannually, under direct supervision of the institute´s staff.

The following compilation is based on results of a guided field excursion to Thessaloniki in September and October 2004. Thessaloniki was chosen as a site of research for a variety of reasons. It has been the focus of various projects by the supervising researcher for almost twenty years, from field work on a former refugee neighbourhood which has by now lost this character altogether (Kokot 1995; 1996), to comparative research on local effects of transformation processes affecting European port cities (2005).

## Thessaloniki restudied

In the context of an earlier study, a group of students from the university of Cologne had already done supervised fieldwork training in Thessaloniki in 1990. The results of this first excursion (Kokot 1990) served as a backdrop for the investigation of transformation processes and their local effects in 2004.

In her study among young members of the Jewish community, Beate Lewkowicz (1990b) had formulated the concept of "private Judaism", which she since has elaborated in further research (Lewkowicz 2006). At the time of her first field work, practicing Jewish religion and identity was in large parts restricted to private events, even when rituals actually were supposed to be performed in public. The trauma of the holocaust and a national ideology of ethnic homogeneity in Greece had caused this caution witin the community. When in 2004 *Sarah Brammann* took up similar questions again, she came to rather different results. While as in 1990, the community is still facing the problem of demographic decrease and mixed marriages are still an issue, today it seems to be far less problematic to reconcile Greek and Jewish identities also on a public level.

It may serve as an indicator of the changes Thessaloniki has been undergoing in the last two decades, that only in the case of the Jewish community the topic of the project in 2004 was directly derived from the 1990 study. The other projects included in this book refer to issues which, at the end of the 1980s, either did not exist at all yet, or seemed to be of marginal importance at that time.

## The concept of "urban subsistence"

From 2002-2006, Thessaloniki was also the site of a collaborative project of anthropologists and NGOs within the EU Community Action Programme (Kokot 2005). This project was based on a comparative investigation of the effects of urban transformation processes on marginalized populations in seven European port cities. Aiming at a joint development of practice programmes and policy recommendations, the ethnographic studies in this project concentrated on the strategies and abilities of marginalized urban groups counteracting the effects of urban change and gentrification. In this context, the working concept of "urban subsistence" was developed, referring to strategies of survival in precarious situations (Kokot, Wonneberger 2006). Extending beyond the economic sector, this concept also includes knowledge and actions relevant to the maintenance of social relations and self-respect.

## Topics and questions

Except for the study in the Jewish community, the concept of "urban subsistence" served as a guideline for designing research topics and questions also for the following studies. Cases range from livelihood strategies among "Russian" street vendors or African women with insecure residence status, to day-to-day transnationalism among Albanian migrants, or the strategic use of social relations among the urban homeless.

While in the earlier project, immigration was still an issue mainly relating to returning labour migrants (Semmler 1990) or political refugees (Jähnig, Vossebrecker 1990), Greece, like other countries of the Mediterranean, has since changed dramatically from a country of emigration to a destination for immigrants. Situated at the borders of the European Union, Greece has become a central entry point for clandestine immigration to the EU. Migrants enter via Turkey, arrive in Thessaloniki from the Greek Islands or pass through the north eastern-borders. While the majority of immigrants today come from Albania and Russia, there is also an increasing influx from Asia and Africa. Consequently, three of five projects described in this book focus on matters of immigration.

Chinese - Greek advertisements in Thessaloniki´s emerging "Chinatown" near Vardar Square (Photo: Kasper de Jong)

In his article on herb vendors in the downtown market area, *Nikola Spilok-Malanda* investigates a very specific economic niche employed exclusively by elderly Russian immigrant women. While female migration has long been neglected in migration studies or treated as an epiphenomenon of lesser importance, recent figures show that in Greece almost half of the immigrants are women (Lazaridis 2000). As *Elke Haas* demonstrates for the case of migrant women from Albania, families in the home countries increasingly rely on the transnational migration of women as a source of economic support. In many cases, women are considered more reliable in their duties to the families and therefore preferred as agents of migratory decisions. This also applies to the African migrant women described by *Kathrin Leven*. Due to restrictions on the Greek labour market and because the often enormous costs of (illegal) migration have to be paid back to the traffickers, some African women must resort to sex work in order to fulfil their ambitions.

For a large part of the public, the increasing number of immigrants to Greece and Thessaloniki is still hard to reconcile with a self-image of Greece as a country of emigration. The increased visibility of homeless people in Thessaloniki is also judged by many as "foreign" or "un-Greek", although in fact, only a small portion of Thessaloniki´s homeless are immigrants. The public display of poverty not only stands in sharp contrast to the restoration and gentrification of large parts of the inner city, but is also widely considered as incompatible with Greek family values. Nonetheless, as *Berit Langeneck* has found, culture-specific forms of sociability (*paréa*) and gender roles also apply to the street culture of the urban homeless, providing support but also limiting their range of options.

## Field work: methods and problems

Ethnographic field methods and techniques of data analysis extending beyond the usual standard of fieldwork, are a core element of the curriculum at the Hamburg institute of anthropology. Courses on systematic observation and questionnaire design, cognitive domain analysis, social networks and qualitative data analysis are offered on a regular basis (Lang 2002; Kokot, Lang 2004). They are considered as prerequisites for the student´s field research projects. In addition to these courses, preparations for this project started more than a year before the actual field work, including seminars on the anthropology of Greece and on Thessaloniki as a site of research, and a seminar on research design. Parallel to these seminars, the students started Greek language classes on a weekly basis, with a private teacher hired on their own initiative. In addition, three of them participated in an intensive summer course offered by the university of Thessaloniki. Aims and topics of research were developed in weekly sessions. Each student provided a research proposal which was continually expanded and redesigned according to the state of preparations, including a detailed work schedule and plan of methods for the field.

Methods of ethnographic field work have been described in detail in various publications. Besides participating in the courses on field methods offered by the Hamburg institute, the compilations by Bernard (2000, 2006) and Beer (2003) were used as main sources for preparing fieldwork.

In the field, the whole group was accommodated in a house in Saranda Ekklisies, a popular former refugee area in comfortable walking distance to most research sites, The owner, a retired teacher, rented amazingly decorated rooms and apartments full of knick-knacks to an ever-changing crowd of guests. The student researchers shared two apartments, while Kokot, who was later joined by her husband, stayed in the one-room "penthouse" on top of the building. Weekly sessions were held on the roof terrace to exchange results and to discuss possible problems, but the close physical proximity ensured a constant flow of communication anyway.

While all topics had been defined far in advance, the first task in the field was to locate suitable units of research. Thessaloniki is a metropolitan city of over one million inhabitants (Thessaloniki Port Authority 2007). Recent immigration has caused massive suburban growth, but many inner city areas are also very densely populated. Our solution was to limit ourselves to a central area (roughly corresponding to the lower city within the historical walls, up to the street Agiou Dimitriou), following experts´ and key informants´ advice in locating the social and spatial boundaries of our research area. Random exploratory walks, and walks guided by key informants, proved to be particularly useful in locating the informants in urban space. Key informants pointed out specific locations, which might have gone unnoticed otherwise. The enclosed map offers an overview of the distribution of our research units in the urban space of Thessaloniki.

Observation of everyday activities, as well as of key events beyond the informants´ normal routine, remain a core technique of ethnographic fieldwork, while the degree of participation in "participant" observation can be quite variable. A characteristic problem of ethnography in urban contexts relates to the limited opportunities of participation in everyday activities. Although all groups studied in these projects could be linked to certain locations, their social relations often reached far beyond the spatial boundaries of our research area. In most cases, close observation was possible only in specific localities or at certain times (as in the soup kitchen in case of the homeless, or at services and official meetings in the case of the Jewish community). The richest data from observation were gained in the case of the herb vendors from Russia, who spent their whole working days in one corner of the central market, where N. Spilok-Malanda could join them and even was appointed some tasks eventually.

Although all students had taken language lessons on a weekly basis for more than a year and were able to communicate sufficiently on an everyday level, in the studies of migrants and in the Jewish community most longer interviews were conducted in English (or Russian in the case of N. Spilok-Malanda). Only B. Langeneck conducted her research on homeless persons exclusively in Greek. Besides longer narrative interviews focusing on life and / or migration histories, field methods included the elicitation of time schedules and, occasionally, free listing for cognitive domain analysis. In almost all cases, the planned elicitation of spatial knowledge by mental maps failed, because informants were obviously unfamiliar with the use of maps or refused to co-operate for other reasons[3].

Although the significance of social networks was immediately obvious and all participants were trained in the elicitation techniques, a systematic elicitation (and analysis) of social network data is missing in all projects. In the cases of migration studies, one reason may be the fear of the informants to divulge information that could endanger their compatriots, whose legal status was insecure. This reluctance was most obvious among the African women interviewed by K. Leven. Presumably because of fear and adverse experiences, some of these women even refused to participate in the study at all. In the case of the Russian herb vendors studied by N. Spilok-Malanda, legal status was less of an issue, but there seemed to be a notable reluctance to impart with business secrets. Officially, there was no agreement on prices among the vendors, but the notable homogeneity of prices seems to be more than just coincidental. Also, claims at a "Russian" or

[3] A similar unwillingness (or disinterest) to read or draw maps was already encountered during Kokot´s research in Kato Toumba (Kokot 1995). Persons who had been living in the area for decades, were not willing / interested to remember street names even in the immediate vicinity, or to draw /show places on maps. However, instead of locating physical structures and boundaries, the same people were very willing and eloquent to define the urban space in terms of social boundaries and social relations ("*this is the place were Maria lives and she is the cousin of Katharina who lives over there*", etc.).

"home-grown" origin of the products might have been jeopardized by more detailed information about the vendors´ network relations.

In the other cases, the reasons for not eliciting systematic network data are less obvious, and seem to be more related to the short time-span in the field. Participant observation provided some important insights, but in order to ask personal questions, moreover in a systematic manner, trust is a major prerequisite. It takes time, however, to build up trustful relationships, and time is limited in a six-week field excursion. Nonetheless, in retrospect it seems that trust was lacking not only on the side of the informants. Some students also did not dare to apply systematic methods because they did not feel comfortable with them, or they feared to intrude on the informants by formal elicitation techniques, without even asking or giving themselves the chance to try. A lesson to be learned from this is to give even more room to the practical application of these techniques during the introductory courses, so students have already some experience in approaching informants and applying these methods, before they enter the actual field.

Data evaluation and writing up the results were the topic of a further seminar in the semester following the field work. Based on the research outlines developed before, topics and questions now had to be adjusted according to the realities in the field and the gathered data. For each project, a series of criteria for evaluation were developed jointly, which also served as a structure for the reports. Qualitative data were evaluated with the programme ATLAS ti[4], using the evaluation criteria as categories for coding. All reports except one[5] were finished until the end of the semester. Four of the participants decided to write their Masters´ theses on subjects related to the field work. Elke Haas and Kathrin Leven have recently finished their theses (Haas 2007, Leven 2007), while Nikola Spilok-Malanda and Berit Langeneck are currently conducting additional fieldwork in Hamburg.

[4] http//www.atlasti.com/de

[5] This delay was due to significant family problems.

## Thanks

Many people have contributed to the success of this project and to the publication of this book. First and foremost, we are greatly indebted to all persons who allowed themselves to be studied, patiently offering not just information, but a great deal of their time. Although their names will not be published in order to protect their privacy, we wish to express our thanks to all of them.

We also owe thanks to the representatives of the Jewish Community of Thessaloniki, and to various NGOs, church-based organizations and associations representing migrants and the homeless. By granting interviews or allowing us to observe and participate in their work, all of them provided invaluable context information.

With her enormous range of contacts in Thessaloniki and her ever-present interest in this project, Salinia Stroux has been a great help to all of us, while preparing the project as well as during field work. Her in-depth knowledge and her unfailing good spirits have been equally appreciated.

While in Thessaloniki, we received substantial academic support from Prof. Eftihia Voutira and her colleagues at Makedonia University. We also thank Prof. Jannis Manos (University of Florina), who visited us in Thessaloniki several times during fieldwork, offering advice and invaluable contacts.

Learning the language in less than one year was definitely one the greatest challenges in this project, but thanks to Stavros Sitaras, all students learned at least enough Greek to communicate sufficiently.

Finally, our landlord in Thessaloniki should not remain unmentioned. Mr. K.´s eminently colourful house in Saranda Ekklisies offered one of the most exciting panoramic views on the port and the Thermaic Gulf to be found in the whole of Thessaloniki. Its abundant decorations and very special atmosphere will provide us with anecdotes and stories for a very long time to come.

# "Hotel Park Bench" close to the White Tower: on being homeless in Thessaloniki

Berit Langeneck

In Greece, homelessness, *anestiótita*, is still regarded as a new phenomenon, "non-typical of the Greek society", and mostly "imported by immigrants" (both Sapounakis 2004:3). This was also the way passers-by and shopkeepers in Thessaloniki commented on this topic during my field work. My research was directed towards survival strategies among homeless men and women. In the following article, I shall focus on the *paréa* of homeless men - sometimes also including women - as a central institution within the spectrum of survival strategies. I will show that social relationships among the homeless were not only important during leisure time in communal drinking and talking, but are also an important source of short-term financial support and exchange of relevant knowledge. Whereas homeless men came together mainly during day time, for homeless women companionship was of particular importance especially during the nights, when they joined men for personal safety when sleeping rough on the park benches or sleeping in hospitals or abandoned houses.

Before describing survival strategies and social relationships, I shall introduce some statistical data about homeless people in Greece and give a short overview of the institutional frame of formal and informal social support in Greece. In this context, I shall also give a brief sketch of the most important institutions for the homeless in the city of Thessaloniki.

## Homelessness in Greece

Although the marginal and precarious way of life of the homeless is taking place in public space, it is hidden from the mainstream of society at the same time. Besides, a definition of homelessness remains difficult (cf. Wolch, Dear 1993:31ff.; Shlay, Rossi 1992:132ff.; Momeni 1990:167ff.; Glasser, Bridgman 1999:2ff.). The *European Federation of National Organisations working with the Homeless* (FEANTSA) offers a typology on homelessness including people who are either roofless (without a shelter of any kind, sleeping rough), houseless (with a temporary place to sleep in institutions or shelter), who live in insecure housing (threatened with severe exclusion due to insecure tenancies, eviction, domestic violence) or live in inadequate housing (in caravans on illegal campsites, in unfit housing, in extreme overcrowding) (FEANTSA 2005:ETHOS).

In regard to Greece, the FEANTSA national report on homelessness criticizes the insufficient registration of the "changing demographic and geographic patterns of homelessness" (Sapounakis 2004:3) by the government and responsible authorities. It is stressed that in Greece, "public debates often ignore the historical link between homelessness, the persistence of poverty, immigration, privatisation of social policies, decentralisation of care, and intensification of social control over marginalized populations that have been documented globally"(Sapounakis 2004:3).

This has resulted in a lack of research and of reliable statistical data. Even though there are some official data about housing, conclusions about housing and homelessness have not been drawn yet, although the Ministry of Health and Social Welfare has organized The National Chart of Welfare including service providers throughout the country, which can give an impression of the fragmented sector of social services. Also the National Statistical Service (ESYE) "have expressed their interest to approach the assessment of the dimensions of homelessness" (Sapounakis 2004:4).

For first-hand data about homeless people in Greece, FEANTSA had to conduct fieldwork considering also homelessness of immigrants, refugees, repatriates and Roma communities. (Sapounakis 2004:3ff.) Their data mainly relate to Athens and the Greater Athens area. In Athens, they identified five urgent-accommodation shelters organised by the state and the municipality. For the region there are sixteen shelters run by the church and twenty shelters organised by NGOs (Sapounakis 2003:19ff.). A description of the services for homeless in Thessaloniki follows below. Based on their fieldwork data, FEANTSA estimates a figure of 17 000 homeless people in Greece, whereas most of them are roofless immigrants, asylum seekers and refugees (8000), 3000 of them accommodated in refugee camps. Approximately another 8000 people, Greek and non-Greek, are accommodated in boarding houses, squatters, institutions and other insecure and transitional accommodations. The number of rough sleepers (Greeks only) amounts to 1000 people (ibid.:18).

## Social Protection and the Greek Welfare State

In their comparative analysis of social policy developments in southern Europe, Rhodes et al. (1997) classified Greece, together with Spain, Portugal and Italy as representative of the southern European welfare model. In this context, Symeonidou outlines that the expenditure on social protection is ranging at a low level compared to other EU members (1997:67ff.)[6]. The family, traditionally and until today responsible for the support in many social realms - often linked to high costs for the family members in charge, especially for women - cannot fill the gap completely (Symeonidou 1997:68).

During the 1950s and 1960s, the emigration of about one million people towards Western Europe and overseas counter-balanced the high unemployment rate, which had been up to 30%. The remissions sent home by the emigrants were a good social provision for their families in Greece. Re-migration in the 1970s also affected the socio-economic realm. The re-migrants strengthened the small business sector by setting up self-contained businesses throughout the country (Symeonidou 1997:69f.).

[6] This is still true for the total expenditure per capita for 2004 (at 1995 constant price, this was also Symeonidou's comparative value ) with 2.73 Euro less than less than half of the EU average (EUROSTAT 2007:16). Regarding the expenditure in relation to each GDP, the expenditures continuously rose from 22% in 1993 to 26% in 2004, whereas the EU average levelled out at 27.6%, starting from 28.7% (for Germany 1993: 27,8%, 2004: 29.5%) (EUROSTAT 2007:14). But more importantly, several authors complain about structural weaknesses, especially due to the socio-economic development of Greece and the resulting delay in construction and insufficient implementation of the welfare regime. They unanimously ask for further reforms (cf. Symeonidou 1997; Apospori 2003). Even though the European Commisson certified "serious effort to extend and improve its social protection system" (Commission Of The European Communities 2003:160), e.g. by improved employability measures and the extension of the Cash Benefit Policy, both in favour of poverty risk groups, critique remains, among others, concerning the remaining high unemployment rate, especially among young and women. Further critique concerns the poverty rate of 20% which is above the EU average of 15% (2001) (ibid.:15, 160).

Considerations about social policy comparable with continental Europe were not undertaken until the re-installation of democracy in 1974. However, relations between citizens and the state remained determined by clientelistic structures, forming a "constraining effect on the development of a collective consciousness and a broad consensus on social policy matters" (ibid.:70). The economic recession of this time, due to the two oil price shocks of 1973 and 1979, slowed down the efforts (ibid.). But still, despite economic problems and high military spending, social protection was improved, e.g. in the beginning of the 1980s, pensions increased to the highest rate in Europe. Simultaneously, the Greek National Health Service (ESY) was established, after the model of the British *National Health System* (NHS). ESY was open to the entire population, providing public health care regardless of the income level.[7]

As described above, pensions were relatively high until the beginning of the 1990s– with 10.6% of the GNP in 1991, compared to7.6% in Germany – and constituted the biggest part of all social protection expenditures (1992: 69%) (Symeonidou 1997:75). The situation of pensioners has worsenend since then. As a comparative study analysing the risk of deprivation and social exclusion regarding different groups in Austria, Germany, Greece, Portugal and the UK shows, retired people in Greece are at much higher risk of income poverty, social exclusion and deprivation than in the northern countries (Apospori 2003:96ff.; Tsakloglou 2003:24ff.; European Commission 2003:24). Sick or disabled people are another risk group for income poverty, with long-term unemployment and lower education as trigger factors. (Apospori 2003:96) Also single mothers with dependent children are at a higher risk of social exclusion, compared to partnered mothers, although in comparison to the other states, this risk is relatively low (ibid.:107ff.; Tsakloglou 2003:26ff.). In the *Greek National Action Plan* (GNAP) of 2001, homelessness was not mentioned as a particular issue (Sapounakis 2004:3).

[7] Plans for the re-organization of financing or more effective processes in public health care have been realized yet (Symeonidou 1997:71f.; Asspospori 2003: 87). At least until the end of the 1990s, corruption in the medical sector was considered part of the treatment (Symeonidou 1997:73). The expansion of the welfare regime in the early 1980s - combined with fragmented structures in the social policy and demographic changes - "brought the system to the verge of collapse" (Apospori 2003:87). Readjustments in the following decade tried to stabilize social policy. As a result, expenditures were reduced. Still, favoritism and clientelist practices are undermining the welfare regime, over-centralization and fragmentation remain inherent in the insufficient structures (ibid.).

Social relations within the Greek extended family remain an important source of support and therefore function as "informal welfare" (Symeonidou 1997:79ff.). Although Apospori (2003:89f) analysed a high level of poverty and material deprivation in Greece, the rate of social deprivation and isolation from neighbours, friends and family was the lowest in comparison with the other countries. Child care, financial support of children's education and the care and financial support of elderly family members is - to a great extent - a matter of the family. Women, as Symeonidou (1997:82) points out, play a central role in taking care of dependent family members.

Even though divorce rates and illegitimate childbirths are at a low level compared to the rest of Europe, there are indicators of a decline of the Greek family, such as decreasing fertility rates or average size of households (Symeonidou 1997:79f.).[8] An important pillar in the "informal" welfare system are the Poor Funds run by the Church of Greece (ibid.:82), as well as services for socially excluded and poor individuals or families including homeless persons, poor elderly people and refugees. Since the 1990s, non-governmental organisations gain increased importance in the sector of welfare.[9]

## Provisions for the Homeless In Thessaloniki

For socially excluded persons like homeless people, the informal institutional welfare provided by the church, NGOs like ARSIS (*Association for the Support of Youth),* and other organisations are the most important sources of assistance. Even if formal services exist, they often do not answer effectively and sufficiently to the needs of the homeless.

[8] Even though there is no explicit family policy in Greece, there have always been material (like subsidies, allowances or tax exemptions) and immaterial (e.g. kindergartens or consultative services) benefits for the protection of the family. Some benefits are provided especially to poor families, immigrants or street children, although provisions and measures are, as in other sectors of social policy, not very high. The number of services is limited, as e.g. the Open Care Centres for the Elderly (KAPI) or public child-care facilities (Symeonidou 1997:76ff.and 78, cf. also Martin 1997).

[9] The Hellenic Red Cross provides services for elderly people and children, especially for orphans (Symeonidou 1997:83). ARSIS´ offices in Athens, Thessaloniki and Volos provide services as well, not only to children at risk (as their main target) but also to the homeless, as described below.

Formal welfare provisions are generally granted only to persons whose documents are complete. In this case it is possible to apply for social benefits. Also individuals who are physically or mentally handicapped by more than 67% can qualify for social benefits, but this has to be proven every two years anew. During my field work, only two of my informants received formal social provisions, both of them suffering from chronicle diseases. For homeless people with an uncertain status like illegal migrants or refugees, or for Greek homeless without complete documents, the barrier for access to social provisions is very high. Many of my informants answered proudly that they were not in need of financial support by the state but could get along on their own. I can not estimate to what extent personal problems like illiteracy or difficulties with bureaucracy and / or the knowledge of the procedures play a role.

In case of a health problem, homeless people can go to any hospital, if they are entitled to welfare payments. All others must refer to NGOs or to doctors who treat patients without documents and for free, but this requires a certain degree of knowledge on how and where to find such a doctor. One of my informants, a rough sleeper roaming the waterfront coast line, tried to take good care of his health and to subsist healthfully, as far as possible. One other man who was transitionally homeless had the necessary papers for admission in case of an emergency. For my other interview partners however, especially for those who were alcoholics and/or long-term homeless, health was not an issue to talk about. They tried to avoid the contact with health care facilities as long as possible.

During my field work in 2004, about twenty soup kitchens run by parishes throughout Thessaloniki were serving not only the homeless, but also poor elderly people and refugees. Meals were served every day except Sunday at noon time, operated by volunteers. In the soup kitchen of Ágion Pánton, which existed since the 1970s, volunteers prepared 150 meals per day. Approximately 30 homeless and up to 40 other needy people queued and picked up the servings. Most of them took the meals away; fewer ate in the courtyard. There were also several soup kitchens run by private bodies throughout the city. In some of them vouchers were required, while others served meals without conditions. One of the private soup kitchens which served meals only once a week was known for its good food, and therefore was very popular.

The municipality provides an emergency shelter for homeless with one four-bed room each for men and for women. These rooms are - as well as sanitary facilities and the office - located at the first floor in the emergency shelter for refugees (*Kéndro Ypodóchis Prosphýgon Thessaloníkis*, briefly *Kéndro*). Rooms for refugees (often families) are in the upper floors. The kitchen and the dining hall are located on the ground floor, where homeless are not allowed to eat, but they can get meals at a soup kitchen next door.

Homeless persons are accommodated in these rooms via the authorities and given a health check up. The duration of the stay is limited to three months, but exceptions in cases of emergency are possible. Greek nationality and complete documents are the most important conditions for accommodation. The *Kéndro*'s front door is locked up for the night, consumption of alcohol and drugs are strictly forbidden. Accidental conflicts arise because rooms do not formally belong to the refugee shelter and because homeless are not allowed to eat in the dining room. For the homeless, this kind of accommodation seems not to fit into their everyday life.

Still, for Eléni, a former homeless woman who had slept rough for three months, the access to the shelter had become a chance. After living in one of the rooms she made the effort to work in the shelter's kitchen, entered into a paid re-employment program and finally got her own room within the building. But, as she points out, she had to try hard; this "success story" is unfortunately a unique one.

Besides the services provided by the municipality, ARSIS also runs a volunteer group of street workers trying to keep contact with the homeless, providing food, clothing and help with bureaucratic matters. Additionally, a social worker can be contacted in the office. It is also possible to just spend some time there and have a coffee.

Compared to the entry procedures for the municipal rooms, the shelter of Ágion Pánton offers access at a low threshold. Entry is granted to everyone in need, except for severe drug consumption or conflicts with the police. Therefore it is quite popular and almost always occupied, in contrast to the rooms in the *Kéndro*, where only two homeless men and one woman were living in the fall of 2004. The shelter of Ágion Pánton is located at the back of the church, 300 meters west of the railway station. The seven rooms lead to the courtyard of about approximately 100sqm, so do the sanitary facilities and the soup kitchen. Several benches surround the place, a big tree provides shadow. In 1996, when the emergency shelter had been established, it was actually supposed to function as short time transitional shelter for people in need of a place, being able to rest some days or weeks before finding work and housing again. Nonetheless, some people stay for months or even years and this is also tolerated.

The courtyard is not only a meeting place for persons who live in the shelter, but also for "visitors": other homeless who come around more or less regularly and spend some time there. In case the shelter is fully occupied, it is also tolerated to spend the night on one of the benches. Apart from the soup kitchen, there are also facilities for receiving some clothes or storing personal properties. The priest in charge tolerates the consumption of alcohol and even drunkenness. To a certain extent, social control is left to the group which is usually present in the courtyard.

## Homelessness and social exclusion

Homelessness is an extreme form of social exclusion. In their comparative study of social exclusion in Europe, Middleton et al. define homelessness

> "not only in terms of income poverty and the lack of material resources, but also in terms of the processes by which some individuals and groups become marginalized in society. They are excluded not simply from the goods and standards of living available to the majority but also from their opportunities, choices and life chances." (Middleton, Barnes, Millar 2003:5)

Homelessness means not only the deprivation from material goods, employment or housing. Becoming homeless also means losing one's social capital, i.e. the social relations or supportive networks of a family, friends or neighbours, providing important functions of social protection.

None of my informants who still maintained some contact with family members received any kind of support from them. To put it the other way: a lack of social networks may not only be a consequence of homelessness, but can also be a reason. When old networks no longer function, the risk of getting homeless rises - particularly among vulnerable people as the poor elderly, ill or drug-addicts.

## Strategies of urban subsistence

To live - and survive - as a homeless person means adapting specific knowledge and new strategies for everyday life, whether one lives on the street or in a shelter. This specific knowledge and everyday strategies - essential in order to cope with precarious conditions, - can be summarized under the concept of "urban subsistence" (Kokot, Wonneberger 2006:2ff.).

The homeless men and women who were my informants during my field work neither belonged to one "circumscribed" group (Underwood 1993; Gruber 2005), nor did they constitute a homogenous group. Nonetheless, certain patterns emerged. Half of my informants were sleeping rough, either at the railway station, or in the parks close to the White Tower and the coast line, the others had found accommodation in the shelter of Ágion Pánton, one woman lived in the municipality's accommodation. Three of my twelve interview partners were women, aged 40 to 50, two of them were former rough sleepers, one of them still lived on the streets. The youngest of the men were about 30 years old, the oldest one, an illegal migrant from Albania aged 75. The duration of their homelessness ranged from one month to 15 years. For some of them it was the first time of being homeless and they considered it just a transitional state, since the perspective for a more or less regular employment was given. For most of the others, homelessness had an episodic character. Times on the street or in the shelter alternated with housing and employment. Approximately one third was born in Thessaloniki and never had been away. Another third had migrated from the rural areas in northern Greece to the city, two people were migrant workers from Albania, one was a refugee from Iraq.

## Income strategies

As described above, only two of the interview partners received welfare payments. One of them was mentally ill, the other one physically handicapped. Most of the others were currently employed as workers or earned a living as day labourers. Others had worked in the past, were currently without work and every day in search of a new job. Typically, they worked as painters or labourers on construction sites, or they found other unskilled jobs like distributing advertisements in the shopping streets. Their working time lasted from two up to twelve hours per day. The earnings were enough for cigarettes, beer and coffee. Only the Albanian migrants told me that they saved some of the money for the future and for the support of their families.

Begging as a strategy of income was considered as undignified. Although there were men and women begging in the streets, my informants explained proudly they were not in such a need and distanced themselves from the beggars. Eléni even claimed that begging was a kind of "hobby" performed by people who actually had enough money, while according to her homeless people did not beg. Nevertheless, money that was given by passers-by without asking for it, was generally accepted. Only one of the Albanian migrants admitted to begging and explained that this way he earned up to six Euro at weekdays and up to twenty Euro at holidays.

## Food, clothing and belongings

At noontime, the homeless of Thessalonki frequent the different soup kitchens of the city for lunch. This meal is in most cases the only food throughout the day. Some of the homeless told me that they just live on coffee and cigarettes on Sundays when the soup kitchens are closed. Small amounts of money are sometimes borrowed from each other for little snacks on Sundays.

Also for clothing, money is not necessarily needed. The shelter of Ágion Pánton and ARSIS distribute used clothes. At Ágion Pánton there are also facilities to change and wash clothes, both for residents of the shelter or for "visitors". Ágion Pánton also provides sanitary facilities, but their use seems to be restricted to residents only. As Athiná, one of the homeless women, told me, at the time when she lived on the streets she used the washing rooms and showers in public sports halls and private gyms or in hospitals, while Stávros went twice a week to a beach south of the city and took a bath in the sea.

Níkos' pangákia at the paralía, in the background one of the first-rate hotels of Thessaloniki (Photo: Berit Langeneck)

The homeless who spent the days at the shelter of Ágion Pánton stored their bags and blankets at a friend's room; other people carried their bags with them during the whole day. Their possessed or carried a varying amount of belongings. Even if most of them were on their way without baggage, one lonely man who roamed the parks at the coast line had a kind of shopping trolley with piled-up blankets and a folding chair with him at all time. Another homeless man, Níkos, who was also on his own at the coast line most of the time, had an old mountain bike with a small trailer where he stored all his baggage after he had aired it on a bench in the morning. Among his things were umbrellas and a sun shade, a folding chair, tarpaulins in case of rain, strings to fix them, a sleeping bag, various bottles with water, cans, various digital thermometers and alarm clocks which he collected, and a big yellow cassette player with radio. He carried these things with him at all times.

## Spending the night

Homeless who were not accommodated in the shelter of Ágion Pánton or in the *Kéndro* spent the nights sleeping rough, in abandoned houses, factories or in car wrecks, often depending on season and weather. Prior to the intensification of the security measures due to the preparations for the Olympic Games in the end of 2003, homeless people also spent the nights in various hospitals of the city where they sneaked in and occupied empty beds. They also used the sanitary facilities there. Athiná, back then spending her time with a group residing at the railway station, had sometimes been allowed to stay overnight in the railway station building, though it had been officially closed both for passengers and for the homeless around midnight. In the end of 2003, when security gates had been installed and homeless people had been banned from the station, her group dispersed and she also had to leave. She tried to spend the nights at the airport for a while, since this is the only public building that stays open throughout the night. Either because of security measures, or because of the relatively long distance of 13 kilometres and an approximately one-hour bus journey to the airport, she slept rough again in the city after some time. None of my interview partners spent the night in somebody else's flat.

Places to sleep rough can be found throughout the city. My informants did not report any restrictions due to the Olympic Games preparations, such as increased police surveillances of the parks and public spaces. As preferred places to sleep rough, the homeless very often referred to the red park benches – *pangákia* - in the city centre, the parks, the forecourt of the railway station and the benches in the courtyard of the shelter of Ágion Pánton. Homeless who owned blankets or even mats, also slept on the green of the parks.

Some men such as Níkos, Stávros and Tákis, spent days and nights on park benches at the coast line around the White Tower and in the parks lining the waterfront southward to Kalamariá. The parks at the White Tower are crossed by gravel walks, trees and bushes stand everywhere on the lawns. This place, with a beautiful sight on the Gulf of Thessaloniki is one of the most popular recreation and meeting points for tourists, residents and street vendors. Around eight o'clock in the morning, the city cleaning staff and gardeners begin their work; some people do their early morning exercise. The place is frequented the whole day through, especially in the late evening and at night. Only after midnight it begins to calm down and the homeless begin to settle for the night.

Further southward down the coast, it is much calmer during day and night. Níkos, who spent most of the day walking at the coast line and most of the nights on one of the benches referred to this calmness and the beautiful view when he explained the choice of his "camp". To others, like Stávros, who preferred the benches in the busier part of the parks around the White Tower, the presence of different people warranted a certain degree of safety. On windy nights, he and other homeless preferred the benches at the railway station, although he described the neighbourhood of the railway station as unsafe and reported that they were afraid that "junkies" would attack them. Some of them even spent every night here. Another advantage of sleeping at the railway station was the closeness to Ágion Pánton, where they had company.

Lévkos Pýrgos, the White Tower (Photo: Berit Langeneck)

Approximately one half of my interview partners were loners who tramped through Thessaloniki, mostly within a fixed territory on routes that followed a certain diurnal rhythm. The other half belonged to the *paréa* (company) of Ágion Pánton, either as residents or as constant visitors, who came along for the daily meal or at night. The main activity in this *paréa* was hanging out in the courtyard, chatting, drinking beer and smoking cigarettes. Two couples from Romania and one Bulgarian, also residents in the shelter, did not participate in the activities at all.

When asked why he spent every night at the railway station although he felt unsafe, Tákis answered that he did not want to be too far away from his *paréa*. Without his *paréa*, he stressed, he would not go anywhere.

## Paréa: a central institution of Greek sociability

*"Paréa"* literally means "company", "companionship", "(circle of) friends", or "clique" (Papataxiarchis 1991:176; Kirtsoglou 2004:5; Pons 2000:450). In his ethnography of male commensality in Aegean Greece, Papataxiarchis describes the *paréa* as a social place where men can have "emotional friendships" (1991:158), which acts as "haven from the troubled waters of kinship" (ibid.:161) and as a source of real, deep, long-lasting emotional friendship. He juxtaposes the concepts of "*paréa*" and "heart-friendship" as male institutions, to the female realm of "family" and "kinship". In contrast to kin structures, a *paréa* is characterized by attributes like "voluntary", "open", "freely terminable" and "egalitarian" (ibid. 176f.). While men cannot easily become friends with relatives, close friendship among unmarried women can grow "in the gaps of matrifocal kinship" (ibid.: 157) as long as there are no domestic obligations. Friendship among married women is seen as "substitute for kinship", is bound to the domestic sphere and "usually fades in time" (ibid.:157f., 161, 175f.).

The male *paréa* meets mostly in the public sphere of the coffee shop (*kafenío*), the "core institution in Greek social life" (Loizos, Papataxiarchis 1991:17), which again is juxtaposed to the "female" domestic realm (ibid.:17f.). The activities of the *paréa* in the *kafenío* include communal drinking, gambling, debating, singing and dancing and are marked by a high level of competitiveness. The egalitarian character of the *paréa* is expressed in symbolic acts like the *kérasma*, which can be translated as "treating someone to a drink" (ibid.: 17; Cowan 1991:188). Being part of a *paréa* is described as an expression of manhood and masculinity[10] (Friedl 1962:87; Cowan 1991:188; Loizos, Papataxiarchis 1991:17; Papataxiarchis 1991:167, 176f.). Comparing several descriptions of *parées*, Kirtsoglou defines *paréa* as

> "a group of people (sometimes specifically male) who come together voluntarily [...], usually in order to enjoy themselves through drinking, eating or dancing

[10] In the case of a *paréa* of gay women in a Greek provincial town (Kirtsoglou 2004), the performance of drinking alcohol and dancing is also linked to the expression of masculinity (ibid.:11). "The girls" in this case study refer to their selves as *paréa*, which constitutes their most important social institution. By conspicuous consumption of alcohol, *kérasma*, food commensality and dancing, as well as by their sexuality, they "negotiate their identity *vis-à-vis* the notions of gender prevalent in the [Greek] society" (Kirtsoglou 2004:2).

but also in other contexts. A paréa can be stable through time and exist beyond the spatio-temporal bounds of commensality or not, while in most cases it is (or it pretends to be) an egalitarian schema" (Kirtsoglou 2004:5).

## The paréa of Ágion Pánton

The composition of the *paréa* of Ágion Pánton was heterogenous and of a temporary character, bound to the place of the courtyard. Two of the residents, Giánnis and Spíros, were long-term homeless men from Thessaloniki, both heavy drinkers, both homeless for about 15 years. Giánnis had been living in the shelter right from the start, helping the priest with smaller works around the shelter and the church. In Spíros' biography, years of homelessness had alternated with times of employment and housing. He had travelled to other countries of Europe when he was working as a cook. He was a relatively new resident, who had been a member of the "railway station group" before. The nights he had spent sleeping rough on benches, in winter time in car wrecks. Before finding accommodation in the shelter, he had spent the nights on the benches in the courtyard.

These two men enjoyed a certain degree of respect, being seniors within the group. Giánnis was the senior resident and, when not heavily drunk, performed some duties in the shelter. Spíros pretended to be a leader and was described by the others as a liar and despot, who let other homeless work for him. Nevertheless, he still received some respect.

Most of the more or less regular visitors were long-term homeless who came around for receiving meals or just to spend time with the others drinking and chatting. The residents and visitors taking part in the *paréa* had become homeless for different reasons. Tákis, an itinerant from Thessaloniki, had lost his documents and was spending the time waiting for replacement sleeping rough and spending the days at Ágion Pánton. It was his first time being homeless and he had the prospect of employment, as soon as his documents were substituted. Edi, a labour migrant from Albania, whose legal status was not yet clear, also had employment and was in search of housing. Asad, a young refugee from Iraq was currently suffering from a neurological disease.

For these men, the *paréa* of Ágion Pánton, meeting every day in the courtyard was the "core institution" of social life. Commensal eating did not play a major role, since food was a rare good served only once a day. United commensality was performed by sitting together, drinking beer and smoking cigarettes, mostly in the mornings, after lunch and in the afternoon. People were coming and going due to their individual rhythms and obligations.

Panagiótis even had two *parées* in the city, one "homeless" of Ágion Pánton and one "non-homeless", a friend he joined at the White Tower. In both cases, he was listening most of the time, only rarely joining the conversation, but drinking and smoking. But he often stressed the fact that he was part of those two *parées*.

The church of Ágion Pánton (Photo: Berit Langeneck)

The entry to the *paréa* was not restricted or ritualised, as Kirtsoglou describes (2004:41). Also, it was not only based on "fellow-feeling" (*simpateía*) (Papataxiarchis 1991:18) but on taking part in the group's commensal and reciprocal activities.

Within the *paréa*, most of the people who had an income shared small amounts of money, beer, cigarettes and sometimes food with those who had no employment. This sharing had the character of general reciprocity since it assured that the person one shared with would probably never be able to give back in equal measure. The shared money was not only intended to fill a shortage, but also to enable the other to perform *kérasma* (e.g. towards myself as a guest or to others in the group). People like the senior resident Spíros, who did not take part in reciprocal activities, were treated carefully and had no good reputation. Spíros was currently working in another district of the city, so he was not at the shelter when meals were served. Although he was not liked, the others, following his instructions, stored his meals for him till he came back from work - opposition was not voiced openly. Besides sharing material things, it was also common to store bags and baggage for people who currently were sleeping rough.

The *paréa* was also a platform not only for the exchange of gossip and news, but also of strategic knowledge. Because of the geographical closeness to the railway station, homeless "newcomers" often approached Ágion Pánton first. For other homeless it was the best place to learn the latest news. An important issue was knowledge about jobs. Asad, who could no longer work due to his illness, "passed" his job to another member of the group. This person shared part of the money not only with his "job broker", but also with other members of the group. Since he knew about possibilities for work at the olive harvest in southern Greece, he took one of the long-term homeless with him and even paid for his train ticket.

## Life's rhythm

The daily life of the homeless is structured by work, services of the shelters and soup kitchens, and by the necessity to find a place to sleep. I shall describe Panagiótis´ particularly regular rhythm of everyday life as an exemplary case:

He was 56 years old and had been homeless since 1990. Seven years later he also lost his employment as factory worker and moved from a town in the east of Greece to Thessaloniki. He was sleeping rough in a woman's company. Every morning he got up at five a.m. One hour later he took a coffee at the kiosk close to the railway station and Ágion Pánton and smoked a cigarette. Around nine a.m. he was asking around for a possibility to work at various places, most of the time without success. At eleven a.m. he arrived in the courtyard of Ágion Pánton where he spent the time with the *paréa* until the meals were served, and also throughout the coming hours. Between four and five p.m. he walked to the White Tower where he spent a few hours at the mobile booth of his friend, who sold nuts and other snacks. There he sat in a folding chair, watched the many passers and listened to the chats they had with the street vendor. Depending on the weather, he went to sleep either at one of the benches at the White Tower or at the railway station around midnight. On Sundays, he was not eating at all because all soup kitchens were closed. Every Wednesday and Saturday, he took the bus to a beach 20 kilometres southeast of the city. During the last years he had spent the relatively cold time from January until April in Kavalla, approximately 150 kilometres east of Thessaloniki. There he could live at a friend's place for free. In return he helped him with the renovation of his house.

Common features in almost all cases were both a high degree of mobility throughout the day, and a relatively regular daily rhythm. Important markers include commitments, the serving of meals or the only leisure time activity: hanging out with friends and *paréa*, chatting, drinking coffee and beer and smoking cigarettes. For the night, almost every rough sleeper left the *paréa* and went to the place he had chosen to spend the night.

## Homeless women

The three homeless women also had a common rhythm of daily activities. Iríni was still sleeping rough, Eléni and Athiná had slept rough before. Throughout most of the day, they spent their time on the streets of the city on their own, without company. At night, they teamed up with a man either for spending the night in a hospital or for sleeping on the benches in the parks, at the railway station or at the *paralía*. For the women, this was a crucial strategy regarding safety and protection at night. In one of these relationships, the man also stored food from the soup kitchen for her and shared his blankets with her. At least in this case, sexual services were given or at least promised in return for nightly protection.

For homeless women who are sleeping rough, teaming up with one or a group of men is a common pattern. Another strategy is finding accommodation in a man's flat, just for one night or for a while (cf. also Novac et al. 1999:7; Passaro 1996:100; Underwood 1993:306). In both cases, sex is the only service the women can give in return, and the threshold to prostitutions is often blurred (cf. Passaro 1996:14, 61-62; Underwood 1993:306).

None of the women, all Greek and aged 40 to 50, talked about having a *paréa* like the men. This can be either be due to the fact that far less women than men were visibly and identifiably homeless. Gender stereotypes also made it more difficult for women to join up among each other. As Kennedy describes for women's friendships on Crete: "Friendship is rare in adulthood, and many women do not have friends. These women explain that other women are untrustworthy, jealous, materialistic, and gossipy" and could be a "threat to their own privacy" (Kennedy 1986:129).

Eléni, who had been successful in leaving the streets, had worked hard to do so. She referred to other homeless women, with whom she had kept company before, as "lazy", "cadger" and "lunatic". Nonetheless, she saw homeless women in general as victims of men or their families, whereas men were "responsible for their own destiny".

Although getting together with men is common, teaming up with another woman for company or protection, or even starting a same-sex relationship, is also known. It has also been described that a "senior" homeless takes a "newcomer" on the street "under her wings" and teaches her what she needs to survive on the streets (cf. Novac et al. 1999:45,51; Passaro 1996:100).

## Conclusion

As shown above, homeless people not only have limited access to formal employment or housing, but also have a lack of social relations within familial or amical networks. Companionship with other homeless people can bridge this gap to a certain degree. Especially for homeless men, the *paréa* of Ágion Pánton was a place where they could spend their leisure time, sitting, drinking and smoking together, talking about the latest news and exchanging knowledge about work and supportive facilities. The group also provided help when baggage had to be stored or food had to be kept safe. Small amounts of money were shared, bridging current financial shortages. Belonging to - at least - one *paréa* was also important for these men in terms of identity. As was proudly pronounced, some even adapted their sleeping places and diurnal rhythm to the place of the *paréa*.

For the homeless women, no such *paréa* existed, even if they occasionally spent some time with the men of the *paréa*. During daytime, women were mostly alone and organized their everyday life on their own. Companionship with homeless men became important during night time, when the women teamed up with men for personal safety. Towards other homeless women, solidarity or friendships did not emerge, and even explicit antipathy was expressed. Homeless women in Thessaloniki have no social relations to non-homeless people and experience similar problems as men in access to formal support, but they are confronted with an even harder struggle in everyday life.

# Vending herbs on the Agora Vlali: strategies of ethnic Greek migrants from the former Soviet Union

**Nikola Spilok-Malanda**

Thessaloniki, in late summer of 2004: an assortment of fresh herbs is displayed on a plastic-box turned upside down. A second box is the vendor's seat. I have her approval to watch her work for a while. I point at a bunch of dill: "This is good for fish." She corrects: "No, no – dill is for potatoes. For fish you need coriander...." She actually sells more coriander than anything else, often several bunches at once. We are talking Russian. Among themselves, the vendors who offer fresh herbs from their simple stalls here at the edge of the market, are speaking Russian too, and also the customers are almost always straightaway addressed in Russian.

The market is the Agora Vlali, a central grocery bazaar, open daily except Sunday. It is located next to the six-lane Egnatia Road, below Platia Dikastirion, where the Odos Aristotelous opens a view down to the sea. Surrounded by higher buildings there is a number of narrow roofed-over streets, in which permanent stands and stores are lined up closely. There are fruiterers and greengrocers, butchers, fishmongers, sellers of olives, cheese and sausages, loudly recommending their goods, which are laid out on counters over the whole front of the store. Other shops can be entered by the customer: here you get spices, sweets or non-perishable foods, small animals and birds are sold as well. There are shops for household goods, for linen, clothing and shoes, devotional objects, toys and souvenirs. While the regular market consists of fixed stalls, the free space on the paths is used by other vendors: some stand in the crowd offering cartons of cigarettes, some stand or squat behind a small box or blanket with reels of thread, lighters or key pendants, others put up a little stall from a blanket, plastic or cardboard boxes or a small table, often completed with a box or chair to sit. This way belts are sold, or sponges and cloths for cleaning, and t-shirts, socks, underwear, spices, cheese, fresh herbs...

This paper deals with Russian-speaking herb vendors on the Agora Vlali, who offered me insights into their working routines by participant observation and conversations. They belong to the group of ethnic Greek migrants from the former Soviet Union, having found a modest chance to earn some money.

The immigration of the "Soviet Greeks" went on recently, in the course of the last 15 years. According to literature, a majority of this group is still facing social exclusion and economic disadvantage (e.g. Triandafyllidou, Veikou 2002:199-201; Halkos, Salamouris 2003:524, 527; Psarrou 2004:72). A strategy to cope with this situation can be the opening of small economic niches. As several sources indicate, trading on markets and flea markets is a "typical" activity, with which the "returnees" are identified by the Greek public (Voutira 1991:408; Spengler-Axiopoulos 2001). However there has been no research focusing upon this topic so far. This study makes a contribution to fill this gap. The general aim of my project was to examine this type of trading activities, which can be regarded as strategies of "urban subsistence" (cf. Kokot, Wonneberger 2006:2-3).

The Agora Vlali was chosen as field site, because a daily market offered more opportunities for a limited period of research than the weekly markets. There I decided to concentrate on the herb vendors, because they were the only case of a whole group of Russian-speaking vendors dealing with the same type of goods. Thus, my field data provide one example of "Russian" vending activity in Thessaloniki that will be described in detail. I shall discuss features of this case regarding its classification as a subsistence strategy, as well as characteristics of this specific economic niche. I propose that herb vending, as a subsistence resource, is based on a culture-specific demand within the migrant group, and bears a part in the manifestation of group identity.

This paper begins with an overview on the historical background of the Pontic-Greek minority in the Soviet Union and some data on their recent migration to Greece. Before proceeding to the main topic, I shall add some other illustrating examples of "Russian" trading activities in Thessaloniki, which might provide a context for this specific case.

## "Russian Greeks"[11]

In recent time, Greece has become a country of immigration, not least since the opening of the East European borders. Among the migrants, the "returnees" or "repatriate Greeks" (according to the official terms) hold a specific position: persons, who by proof of their Greek descent are granted Greek citizenship (Kokkinos 1991a:314; 1991b:395-399; Stathakis: 2002b:76-77, 79-84)[12]. In the immigration law 1975/1991, especially the "Albanian Greeks" ("*Vorioepirotes*") and the "Pontic returnees" as "*omogenés*" are separated from "foreign" immigrants because of their Greek origin, though a definition of "*omogenís*" is not given. Triandafyllidou and Veikou quote a decision of the higher administrative court for characterization of this term: „...'to belong to the Greek Ethnos'. That is, 'to have Greek national consciousness', which is 'deduced from characteristics of personality which refer to common descent, language, religion, national traditions and extensive knowledge of the historical events of the nation'" (Triandafyllidou, Veikou 2002:198). A presidential decree from 1983 furthermore granted the Pontic Greeks the right to "return to their homeland", Greece. All in all it seems that the "Pontic returnees" enjoy a preferential treatment regarding their legal status and the processing of their application (Triandafyllidou, Veikou 2002:198).

The Greek minority in the USSR consisted mainly of Pontic Greeks (Voutira 1997b), who are named after their original settlement area at the coast of the Black Sea, where

[11] Since matters of identity were not a central question of this study, I did not ask explicitly whether the herb vendors considered themselves to be "Russians", "Russian Greeks", "Pontic Greeks", "Russian-speaking Greeks", "Georgian Greeks", etc.... I chose my informants based on their occupation and the Russian language, while the nationalities stated in their passports are irrelevant to my research (actually all of them had come from Georgia). I am aware of the possible negative connotations of the term "*rossopóntioi*" in Greece, which can also apply to referring to a person as "Russian". Nevertheless I decided to use this term whenever the context requires an emphasis or differentiation, e.g. in "Russian" vendors. This is not to be understood as an expression of national belonging, let alone as pejorative, but only in the neutral sense of "Russian-speaking".

[12] The Greek constitution according to art. 1, § 3 and art. 108 in general grants a privileged legal status in Greece to members of the Greek diaspora, if they as immigrants declare and prove their Greek origin. In this case they are legitimated as de facto refugees or "*omogenés*" = "of same descent"; Triandafyllidou and Veikou translate the term with "co-ethnics"; it is also generally used to refer to "Greeks abroad" (PONS 2000). For a detailed discussion of the particular terms, including „refugee" as a positive self-ascription, which has in the meantime become officially accepted, see Voutira 2003b.

archaeological evidence proves Greek settlements since the 8th century BC. Distant from the Greek heartland developed a distinct Pontic culture and the Pontic dialect, which is hardly understood in Greece today (Kokkinos 1991a:313; Bryer 1991:316-25). Since the end of the 18th century migration increased from the Ottoman Empire to the south of the Russian territory, directly following the explicit call of the Russian tsars, who supported the settlement of peasant and mining workers. The growing trade- and sea-port-cities also attracted merchants and workers. During the Russian-Turkish wars, Greeks fled the Ottoman Empire in fear of repressions after having supported the Russian side. After 1828/29, Greeks migrated into the Caucasus. The mountain region of Tsalka became a nearly homogeneous area of Greek immigrants. At the beginning of the 20th century, the total number of Greeks on Russian territory is estimated 650,000, 2/3 of which were rural population (Bryer 1991:326-327; Stathakis 2002a:53-54). Rising nationalism in the Young Turks movement and the Greek-Turkish war of 1919-22 also drove further refugees to Russian territories[13].

In the beginning, the young Soviet Union pursued a decidedly liberal minority policy, which even led to the creation of three autonomous Greek regions in South-Ukraine and the region of Kuban (Xanthopoulou-Kyriakou 1991:362; Karpozilos 1991:365; Stathakis 2002a:55; Agtzidis 1991:373). Under the rule of Stalin, this course was reversed – like other minorities the Greeks were subjected to repressions and mass deportations to Siberia and Central Asia. (Agtzidis 1991:374-377; Stathakis 2002a:55-56,). After the Greek civil war, the Greek state showed little interest in receiving those Greeks willing to leave the Soviet Union. After the relaxation of minority policy under Khrushchev, Pontian organizations in the USSR in the first place, spoke up for the right to return to the former settlement areas and for restitution of expropriated possessions (Agtzidis 1991:377; Stathakis 2002a:56). With the perestroika the number of Pontian associations, cultural centres, newspapers and schools strongly increased, especially in the "regions of origin". In 1989 an "All-Union association of Greeks in the USSR" was founded.

[13] By this time Greece experienced a wave of 1.5 million refugees from Asia Minor and the Pontos, who were fleeing from the war and finally resettled in the course of the population exchange between Turkey and Greece in 1923. Greece´s coping with this "catastrophe" is today seen as a "national victory". The refugees, marginalized at first, quickly assimilated in the Greek society. Particularly the Pontians are considered as a "success model" (see e.g. Hirschon 1989, 2003: 3-8; Kokot 1995, 1996, Voutira 1991: 406, 1997a: 117-119; Vergeti 1991: 384-385).

In 1990 there were negotiations with Yeltsin about the establishment of an autonomous Greek republic at the Black Sea coast (Agtzidis 1991:379-380; Stathakis 2002a: 57-58).

In today's Russia, Ukraine and Georgia, the Greeks are officially recognized as an ethnic minority. A census in 1989 came to a total number of 350 000, 2/3 of which indicated a different language (mainly Russian) as their mother tongue (Mark 1989:entry „Griechen“; Kozlov 1988:187). Because of the adoption of other nationalities, also due to a lot of "mixed marriages", Pontian associations estimate the number of Soviet Greeks at that time to be from 500 000 up to one million (Stathakis 2002a:58).

A major wave of "Soviet" Greek migration took place in the 1990s. From 1300 persons in the year 1988 the number increased tenfold to the next year and reached its climax in 1993 with 20 000. Official data amount to 120 000 to 150 000 for the years 1989-1997; among these (due to the unstable situation) were about three quarters of the Greek population of the Caucasus. Unofficial estimates still assume a total number of more than 700 000 migrants from the territory of the USSR, as unreported cases not registered by the "returnee-visa" are to be added (Kokkinos 1991a:314; 1991b:395-399; Stathakis: 2002b:76-77, 79-84).

To some extent, the Greek state seems to have been taken by surprise by the sudden increase of immigrant numbers. After provisional arrival camps, it was intended to canalize the masses by building- and settlement projects (which were altogether not fully sufficient) and to support their integration by language- and educational programs (Kokkinos 1991a:314; 1991b:395-399; Stathakis: 2002b:76-77, 79-84; Triandafyllidou, Veikou 2002:199). The official rhetoric tried to revive the "successful coping with the refugee situation of 1923" (Voutira 2003a:146-157). According to official data, there was a total of 155 319 "repatriates" in the year 2000, one-third of them were registered in Thessaloniki alone. In the whole North of Greece lived 59% of the "returnees", 22% in Attica and Athens (Spengler-Axiopoulos 2001; Voutira 2004; cf. also Kiprianos et al. 2003:150).

Despite the positive rhetoric on the part of the state, the "Pontian returnees" were hardly accepted by the public as "Greeks returning home". Instead, they were marginalised as "*rossopóntioi*"[14] or simply as "Russians". Although they are claimed to have received special privileges, this only applies in comparison to other, particularly illegal, migrant groups (Triandafyllidou, Veikou 2002:199-201)[15]. According to a study by Halkos and Salamouris (2003) who recorded statistical data of 6994 Pontic returnees in Western Athens, the main motivation for migration was not the economic situation, but an identification with Greece as their "home country". 43% of the respondents stated that their financial situation was worse than before "repatriation", 34% indicated it as unchanged. A total of 35,6% were without job, 2/3 of these were women. Among the younger immigrants, the unemployment rate was above this average, just as among those with a higher education level (Halkos, Salamouris 2003:524).

As it seems, the "Soviet Greeks" aroused a special scientific interest only during the first migration wave in the 1980s and their arrival in Greece. A main focus then was directed towards the question of identity, considering the paradox of the "return" of a diaspora, which had already existed before its home country was founded (e.g. Voutira 1991; 1997a; 2003a; Deltsou 2000; Hadjitaki-Kapsomenou 2001)[16]. As for more recent publications, it seems that the Russian Greeks or "new" Pontians are mentioned in studies on the general situation of immigration in Greece, while the main interest increasingly turns towards illegal migrants of other origins.

[14] This term has soon earned a pejorative connotation, as it stresses the foreign origin of the "Russian Pontians" and has become connected with stereotype prejudices.

[15] Fundamental data on financial aid policies is provided by Psarrou (2004). When arriving in Greece, each "repatriate" received a (rather symbolic) sum of about 120 Euro for initial settlement, together with about 175 Euro for each family for the transportation of their belongings (Psarrou 2004: 13). In the context of this paper the situation of elderly people is of special importance. Psarrou points out, that there are still no bilateral agreements between Greece and the FSU, which means that the Pontians lose their pension claims when emigrating (Psarrou 2004: 25, 71). In Greece they get a pension of 44 Euro per month from a public insurance agency (OGA) plus about 4,5 Euro from the Welfare Office, which does not even cover the expenses for a half month's food (Psarrou 2004: 13, 72). At least the repatriates are eligible to free medical and pharmaceutical care from public hospitals (Psarrou 2004: 13). They also enjoy tax exemptions, which allow them to sell clothes, furniture, household appliances etc. they brought with them without paying any duties (Psarrou 2004: 14). This surely facilitated the rise of "Russian" flea market activities that are described in the next section. Psarrou again underlines the fact that these privileges are granted only to those who went through the legal procedure of "repatriation" (2004: 14).

[16] A comprehensive overview is given in a special issue of the *Journal of Refugee Studies* (1991, 4/4).

## "Russian" traders in Thessaloniki: first impressions

The following description is based upon impressions gained while looking for an appropriate field, and by research in the vicinity of the Agora Vlali. It does not claim to represent an exhaustive picture, but it might give an impression of the variety of "Russian" trading activities, for which herb vending is but one example.

Apart from the central market area to which the Agora Vlali belongs, farmers' markets are set up in various residential quarters on different days of the week. The big market taking place on Wednesdays around the Rotonda[17] is a good example for what is meant by the popular expression "Russian flea market". Attached to the regular market with fruit and vegetables, foodstuffs and houseware, there is a large number of informal stands whose vendors are speaking Russian. Their goods range from clothes, shoes, cloths and handbags to buttons, books, stamps and coins, from used cameras, jewellery and haberdashery to rummage, knick-knack and souvenirs. Many of the second hand items tell their origin by Cyrillic labels. Reaching out into the side streets, the stands become more and more simple. Near the centre, the vendors drive up with their cars and build up solid stands of desks and canopies, while at the fringes the goods are displayed on the ground.

"Russian" flea market stand (Photo: Salinia Stroux)

Platia Dikastirion is located above the Agora Vlali on the other side of the Egnatia, in one line with Odos Aristotelous (Aristotelous Street). This is a spacious square with broad paved footpaths, trees, benches and some

[17] The Rotonda is one of the historical monuments of Thessaloniki. The large cylindrical building was erected in 306 A.D. under Caesar Galerius, presumably to be his mausoleum. Having served as a Christian church since the 4th century it was turned into a mosque in Ottoman times when a minaret was added. Today it is the Orthodox church of Agios Georgiou.

spaces of green. On the upper side is a children's playground. Several informants indicated that this square can be regarded as a "Russian" meeting place. During the day, elderly men gather here, to talk in the shadow of the trees and to play cards. In the evening, it turns into a meeting place for families with children. One cannot fail to notice the number of "Russian" shops here. Most of them are located at the north-western side of the square in Odos Venezielou. There are two groceries; one of them, according to the shop man, nine years ago was founded as "the first Russian shop in all Greece". There is a bookshop, just celebrating its sixth anniversary, a newly opened video shop, a translation bureau, travel- and money transfer agencies. At the north-eastern side (Odos Filipou) there is another travel bureau, displaying in its window an announcement in Russian that parcels are being taken abroad every Monday, as well as a note concerning graveyard care in Georgian villages. A further shop in Filipou Street is dealing with Russian books, magazines, music, videos and some souvenirs. It was established four years ago. Its owner offers a part of his repertoire at Rotonda and other weekly markets. In another side street (Ioustinianou), there is a third grocery shop that was opened seven months ago. Most of its "Russian" goods were produced in Germany. In front of the biggest grocery, I frequently met an old man from Moscow, who was hoping for Russian-speaking customers as well: in a suitcase, fixed to his bicycle's carrier, he had a collection of feature films, which he records via satellite from Russian TV. Additionally, he sells sunflower seeds.

Asking whether this was a "typical" residential area, I several times got the reply that indeed "Russian Greeks" were living around here, but in fact they were spread throughout the whole municipal area, but all would come here for shopping.

As my actual research site was confined to the Agora Vlali, I did not survey Russian shops in other quarters of the city. By occasion, I noticed some Cyrillic shop signs in Agia Dimitrou.

On the Agora Vlali itself, I soon recognized that the herb vendors were not the only ones who were speaking Russian. So did not only other "mobile" vendors, but also shopkeepers of regular stands. My impression was that these shops concentrated in that part of the market, where the herb vendors had their usual places, too. A permanent green grocer's stand had been run by "Russian Greeks" for four years.

## Herb vending on the Agora Vlali: features of an economic survival strategy

As already mentioned in the introducing description, the herb vendors do not fit the regular concept of the Agora Vlali, which consists of solid permanent shops and stands. Instead, they belong to the kind of vendors who join the market with little makeshift stalls. According to its ways and extent this occupation can be regarded as a subsistence strategy, as will be shown in the following portrait. In view of this approach, I shall first illustrate some particular aspects of this economic strategy.

The minimal equipment of an herb vendor's stall is a plastic or cardboard box, turned upside down, on which the goods are displayed. Presumably this is necessary, since it would be unfavourable to present foodstuff right close to the ground. Most of the vendors also use a seat, usually a second box, sometimes a chair. Two vendors, who appeared only once, respectively twice, for an afternoon, did the selling standing up.

The goods and all accessories are brought along in plastic bags. Further accessories include polythene bags (to put the goods in for the customers), rubber bands (to bundle up the herbs), and occasionally a spray-bottle with water (to keep the leaves fresh).

There are different strategies of setting up and removing the stalls. Some vendors provide the boxes and cartons from market stands or from the places where empty packaging material is collected for the refuse disposal, and return them when finishing work. Others bring and take them along. In one case, I was invited to help with hiding a vendor's equipment somewhere not too far away from the market.

Among the fresh herbs offered regularly, coriander leaves ranked in the first place. They were always selling well, often by several bunches to one customer. Also spring onions and basil, often parsley and dill, less frequently roquette, small radishes or oregano. Everything was sold by bunches at prices of 70 - 50 Cent. Usually, at least three different kinds of herbs were offered. Only occasionally single vendors expanded their repertoire, for instance by a home-made red seasoning sauce filled in bottles or several spice powders (amongst others onion, saffron, coriander), which could be mixed for tzatziki dip and were measured by a small glass at 1 Euro each.

As for the origin of their goods, vendors gave different information. Some said that they were buying them, which they also told to the customers to explain the comparatively high prices. Others declared that the herbs were home-grown. This also served in sales talk as an argument for the price and quality of the products, which were praised to be "fresh and without dirt".

Most of the herb vendors were women of pensionable age. During our five-week stay only four men appeared in order to sell herbs, three of them just sporadically. The other vendors were women at the age of about 50 and older. All of them spoke Russian and except for one, they had all emigrated from Georgia. To find a job after migration to a foreign country is in most instances not easy. With advanced age, it surely becomes even more difficult. Thus herb vending serves as an economic niche for those whose chances on the regular labour market are minimal. From my field data, I estimate that an herb vendor's gross earnings might come up to 30-50 Euro a day. There was only one woman who worked almost every day and all day long. In her case one could presume, that she could possibly manage to earn a very modest living from this occupation, since she might at least reach the Greek statutory national minimum wage, which in 2004 was 631 Euro for employees (Statistisches Bundesamt 2007:6). Still this is far from the average workers' monthly net wage of about 1140 Euro in 2004 (Statistisches Bundesamt 2007: 10) and rather corresponds with the poverty threshold which is usually fixed at 60% of the national median income (cf. European Commission 2004:17). For the majority of the vendors, who worked less often, it is to be presumed that the extent of their occupation rather allows them to "earn a bit of extra money", as one women herself named it. For somebody who had to support a family the earnings from the niche of herb vending surely would be insufficient.

I cannot judge how well the vendors knew Greek. Presumably, many of them had learned it only after their arrival in Greece, and if at all, previously had spoken only the Pontic dialect. In any case, in this occupation they were able to fall back on their other language skills, mainly Russian, which most of the customers also were speaking.

I never met one of the herb vendors dealing with other goods, nor was such practice mentioned in our conversations. One woman, who got the herbs from her son's garden, told me she would not sell in winter, but right now the crop was sufficient to go to the market once a week. Provided that the vendors have specialized only in selling fresh herbs, this means that their economic strategy is based on particular resources, which allow them to earn a little money in a small and clear-cut niche. To summarize, herb vending on the Agora Vlali can be identified as an economic survival strategy of Russian-speaking migrants. In particular, it is used by elderly women to contribute to the household budget. The components of the stalls and further equipment can undoubtedly be obtained on lowest expense. As far as the herbs are home-grown, this is a possibility to reduce costs to a minimum since time, rather than money has to be invested.

My data indicate that herb vendors did work with different frequency: few worked almost every day, others once or twice a week, again and again a new face joined the group, some appeared just once. Nevertheless, some common patterns in the work routine became visible: In contrast to the regular vendors on the market, who loudly praise their goods, call out prices and talk to every passer-by on first eye-contact, the "Russian" vendors acted very unobtrusively. As a rule they kept sitting quietly, looked at the people walking by and waited until customers approached them. If passes-by were approached, they were directly spoken to in Russian. A continual occupation was to look through the goods and pick withered leaves and stems. Some kept the herbs fresh by spraying them with water. Sold bunches also were to be immediately replaced, since a large part of the goods were not displayed, but kept in plastic bags behind the "counter"-box. One vendor had brought along his herbs assorted but loose in a large bag and used the time till he finished work to bundle everything with rubber-rings. On the ground of the bag he had put some water to keep his goods from withering.

Two of the women, who told me that they were buying their goods, had brought their herbs along in larger bunches, of which they on the spot made several smaller ones to sell. Greiner (2003:76) mentions this strategy of "fractioning goods in small and smallest units" as a characteristic of street vending. His explanation corresponds with my own reflections: one result is to raise prices for the end consumer; another effect lies in the possibility to adapt to varying consumer demands.

In the meantime, dropped leaves and stems were raked together to keep the stall clean all the time. After work, the spot was carefully cleaned up and all rubbish was thrown into the dustbin. When a vendor had left, no trace remained to tell that only just somebody had been selling herbs in this place. These actions were carried out by all vendors with the same thorough routine, by those who were working daily as well as by those whom I met only once. Everyone was prepared to hand the herbs to the customers in small polythene bags. Also the size of the bunches sold always remained the same. The vendors always had enough change ready. Surplus receipts and banknotes were put away in a separate purse. One woman, who worked daily, checked her earnings in a little book.

In contrast to the regular market stands, prices were never displayed in any way. The vendors started in the morning with 70-80 cents and lowered prices to 50 cents in the course of the day. This was also mentioned in sales talk: "a while ago I sold it for 70 cents." They never let themselves in for any haggling, except immediately before finishing their work, in order to sell off the last bunches. All vendors sold at the same price and did not let themselves be put off by customers, who claimed that on the other corner the herbs were cheaper. In any case, their prices were higher than in the market stands, where a bunch of parsley was sold at 30-40 cents.

Herb vending on the Agora Vlali (Photo: Salinia Stroux)

The herb vendors did not show any open competition. If they were sitting together in a line, no one tried to call a customer away from the others. On the contrary, in sales talk they also praised such goods of their neighbours they did not offer themselves. Sometimes you could even hear them say: "Hand me two bunches of spring onions – I just sold them for you..." Beyond that there was another level of cooperation, which I could not fathom in its completeness: Obviously the vendors exchanged part of their goods or handed some of them on to each other. The following examples gave evidence of this strategy: One woman who stopped her selling asked me to watch her stall for a while and then little by little took away all her goods into the market. I presume that she brought them to the vendors on the other corner. Another woman told me that the herbs were all grown in her son's garden, except for the spring onions, which she got from the woman sitting next to her. Even though I did not understand the whole background of these strategies, they show relationships reaching beyond mere neighbourhood or competition.

## Coriander: a culture-specific demand?

As has been shown, the niche of herb vending on the Agora Vlali was exclusively used by Russian-speaking migrants.[18] As mentioned in the introducing description, there were other mobile vendors on the market offering cigarettes, belts, socks, sponges or sewing thread. At first glance, fresh herbs belong to this type of "neutral" goods, which anybody can sell or buy, but in the following part of this paper, I shall expand on the thesis that "Russian" herb vending is an economic niche strategy based on culture-specific demand.

Inquiries on farmers' markets and in the neighbourhood of the Agora Vlali confirmed market vending to be a typical strategy used by migrants from the former Soviet Union (cf. Voutira 1991:408; Spengler-Axiopoulos 2001). A large number of vendors could be "identified" from the goods they offered: Russian videos, Russian household remedies, Russian sheet calendars, Russian flea market items like books, badges, postcards, cameras and razor blades with Cyrillic labels, and so on. The shops around the Platia Dikastirion also undoubtedly address a "Russian" clientele.

As far as the herb vendors are concerned, not only did they without exception speak Russian, but so did the far majority of their customers, too. It seemed to be no question

[18] There is evidence however, that fresh herbs were sold on Greek markets in earlier times as well. In his survey on markets in Thessaloniki, Wiebe (1978:242-43) recorded some stands with potted herbs and classified the vendors as "self-marketers". In the 1940s and 50s, street vendors with donkeys loaded with wild greens were a common sight in Athens. They have long disappeared, but elderly country people still gather wild greens and occasionally sell them on farmers' markets to earn some pocket money (Kitrilakis, Kitrilakis 2001:134).

to both vendors and customers to approach the other straightaway in Russian. The vendors at the entrance of "Aristotelous" were frequently joined by two elderly women who were selling homemade cheese. This was a speciality from their previous home country – Georgia.

The best-selling herb was coriander. My presumption that there might also be an explicitly ethnic background for coriander was confirmed by an internet search[19] for Georgian recipes. Fresh coriander is frequently used as an ingredient and I repeatedly found the explicit statement that coriander is *the* typical seasoning of the Georgian cuisine. In a Georgian cookbook (Hildebrand 2005), coriander is an ingredient in 362 out of 542 dishes (soups, hors d'oeuvres, fish-, meat-, poultry-, vegetable-, mushroom- and egg-dishes). The red seasoning sauce and the mixed spices two vendors added to their repertoire, can be expected to be Georgian as well.

The parts of the mosaic fit together: customers from Georgia buy ingredients from vendors from Georgia for typical Georgian dishes. Thus, herb vending is a market niche based on a culture-specific (i.e. specific "Georgian") customers' demand. Although coriander is not unknown in Greek cuisine, it is surely not a typical spice. The Russian-speaking herb vendors from Georgia recognize this specific demand and are ready to cover it. The relatively high number of migrants from Georgia as potential customers makes this specialisation both possible and worthwhile.

If herb vendors on the Agora Vlali cover a "group-specific" market niche, this also offers an explanation for their restrained sales behaviour. If their main target group is defined in advance, it makes not much sense to praise their goods in Greek, nor to approach every passer-by in Russian. Speaking Russian thus appears to link with the complex of a specific market niche. It corresponds with the cultural background of the offered goods, and thus plays more than a pragmatic role in the vendors' interactions with the customers. Since sales talk and additional chats in Russian or Georgian is identified with this type of business, it would be difficult for a non-Russian-speaking vendor to set up in this niche. It might even be a further motivation to the customers to support needy fellow

[19] http://www.georgien.net/Esstrink/esstrink.html; http://www.kimeraweb.de/essen/kueche.html http://www.georgien.net/shop/georgischer-kaese.php; [11.03.2005]

"countrywomen" by their purchase. Still, the herb vendors are meeting a very specific demand, providing their customers with an essential ingredient for the familiar cuisine they brought with them. In this sense, herb vending fulfils the purpose of maintaining an ethnic food culture, which is a manifestation of Georgian-Greek identity. As Mennell et al. point out, „... immigrants and ethnic minorities try to maintain their own cooking and eating habits as long as possible..." (1992:78).[20]

## Conclusion

Greiner (2003) characterises street vending by the use of urban public space as a selling area, while spatial mobility is of some importance. In this regard, street vending is opposed to institutionalised market trade as well as to shop sales, while degrees of overlapping might be still possible (Greiner 2003:4-5).

In the case described in my paper, herb vending is largely tied to the Agora Vlali. On the reasons for this I can only speculate. Possibly, the Agora Vlali, which attracts customers being a central daily food bazaar, is particularly favourable to the herb vendors.

The minimum equipment of the stalls, which could be brought and taken away by one person on foot, is typical for street vending. This impression is supported by the fact that that they do not correspond with the market's regular concept of solid stands and shops. On the other hand, there are always quite a number of vendors with "mobile" stalls on the Agora Vlali. The herb vendors go in line with this practice and are not a complete exception. Their stalls, by the way, were even less suitable to pack up and disappear within a moment, than were those of some other vendors. I also never witnessed that they were checked for a licence. All in all, their occupation takes an intermediate position. According to the place it is market trade, while technically it shares aspects of street vending.

[20] A discussion of the relationship between ethnic cuisine and identity is contributed by Van den Berghe (1984) and by Sutton (2001:73-86). Goddard (1996:213) and Kravva (2001) also deal with the role of food as an element, marker and expression of identity and refer to its meaning for personal as well as for collective memories. An interesting parallel to the case discussed here can be found in Sutton (2001:73-74, 84): as an example he mentions that fresh basil serves as a symbol of home and identity among members of the Greek diaspora.

In the analysis of street vending, a distinction has been drawn between mobile vendors, i.e. those who keep moving with their goods, and vendors with mobile stands who yet set up stationary for a time in one place. In the latter sense, the herb vendors are mobile as well, which leads to several aspects of flexibility. Although they apparently seem to keep tied to the Agora Vlali, they are still mobile in this place, i.e. theoretically they would be able to decide every day anew where to put up their stalls. In practice, they work as a rule at two usual spots and just occasionally take up another place.

The mobility of their stalls gave the vendors flexibility in different ways. As an economic survival strategy on which one might fall back sporadically at low investment costs, it would be unfavourable to keep up a permanent shop, but open it only for some hours a day, once a week, or even less frequently. Provided that the vendors are growing the herbs themselves, selling can be adapted to their own garden's "productivity". The mutual cooperation in exchanging and handing on goods also contributes to increased flexibility.

In the preceding description, I described herb vending on the Agora Vlali as a survival strategy within a specific economic niche, occupying an intermediate zone between market trade and street vending. Most of the actors are women of pensionable age. This implies that this occupation is chosen for a lack of other job opportunities. I also propose that this niche is based on a culture-specific demand, based mainly on coriander as an essential ingredient of the familiar cuisine the migrants brought with them. Generally, herb vending is part of the "Russian business" on the Agora Vlali and in its surroundings, covering a significant and special customer's demand.

# African Migrant Women in Thessaloniki

**Kathrin Leven**

Since the beginning of the 1990s Greece has developed to a country of immigration for approximately one million people, most of them searching for better working conditions and better chances in life. The majority comes from Albania and Eastern Europe, but migration from Asian and African countries is increasing.

For a long time labour-migration has been regarded as a male phenomenon, while women have been described mainly as wives accompanying the men. Current studies show however that nearly half of the African migrants to Greece are women, entering on their own and as the sole providers for their remaining families in Africa. The conditions of female migrants are of interest both to Greek science and society, although most studies focus on the numerical majority of women from Albania and Eastern Europe. However, African women migrating to Greece are confronted with realities that differ significantly from those of their male compatriots and also from those of the female European migrants.

During my fieldwork in 2004, I examined the conditions of life and work of African women in Thessaloniki, the largest port-city in the north of Greece. This study is based on ten key informants' biographical background, their reasons for migration, aims and hopes, actual living conditions in Thessaloniki, their strategies to deal with these conditions, their transnational relationships and their plans for the future. Most of these women had achieved qualifications in Africa, so they did not only look for a well-paid work with which they could support their family at home, but also for opportunities to put their abilities into practice, or to obtain secondary education and a further career. These cases show that the European stereotype of the unqualified African migrant trying to escape existentially dangerous poverty and warlike disturbances, does not apply to all cases.

In this article I shall examine the extent to which the African women are able to implement their aims. Introducing, I shall give a short outline of the migration history of Greece, developing from a country of emigration to an immigration country, as well as of the political and social conditions for migrants, especially in Thessaloniki. The following section is predominantly based on empirical data, starting with a description of the research field, pointing out locations that are important for the African population in Thessaloniki. Subsequently, the key informants and their migration backgrounds and aims are introduced. Describing the working conditions of my informants, I shall also point to the employment of African women in the sex industry and the migration networks through which they enter these occupations.

## Women´s migration to Greece: state of research

Although there is a great deal of literature on migration and even on the global increase of female labour migration, sources on the very recent history of African women in Greece are scarce and problematic. In most works on Greece, the authors deal with the relatively new phenomenon of immigration to Greece, focusing on migrants from Albania and the former Eastern Block, as well as on reactions in Greek society.

In her article *Greece and its New Immigrants* (2002), Jutta Lauth Bacas describes the migration history of Greece and the status of different immigrants. She also investigates attitudes and practices of Greeks towards the new immigration. Fakiolas (2000) also deals with the development of Greece to a country of immigration and with the regional, social and economic pull-factors, making Greece an explicit destination for immigrants.

In most works on the specific situation of female migrant labourers in Greece, female migrant labourers are inevitably seen as victims of sexual exploitation, who can make a living only by working in the sex industry (Phizacklea 2000; Psimmenos 2000; Karakatsanis, Swarts 2003; Lazaridis 2001). In these reports, the specific situation of African migrant women in Greece is treated only marginally, although my empirical data suggest that they are exposed to enhanced racist reactions due to their skin colour. It should be noted that I could only revert to literature in English or German, because of my insufficient knowledge of Greek. Possibly there are more publications on this topic in Greek, but since most Greek authors publish in English, my assessment of the state of research should be realistic.

## Greece as a destination for migrants

Like other Southern European countries such as Spain, Portugal and Italy, Greece developed from a traditional country of emigration to an immigration country in the 1980s. From the end of World War II until the middle of the 1970s, approximately one million Greeks left their country because of economical reasons. Nearly half of them have returned since 1974. In the 1980s, a considerable number of immigrants from Poland and developing countries came to work in Greece for the first time. Until the end of the 1980s, the number of immigrants had been under 50 000 people; changing dramatically in the 1990s, with immigration primarily from Albania and from Eastern Europe, but also from Asia and Africa (Fakiolas 2000:58f.).

After official estimates, 800 000 to one million migrants lived in Greece in 2002 at a total population of about 10.3 million. Regarding these estimates Greece shows the highest immigration rate of the EU (Tastsoglou, Hadjicostandi 2003:193). The proportion of legal to illegal immigrants is estimated at one to five. Most migrants enter illegally via land or sea borders or they enter Greece with a tourist visa and remain in the country after the expiration date (Lauth Bacas 2002:199f.). The state reacts with rigorous deportation of all illegal migrants who are caught, but they usually try to return to Greece by another way. From 1994 until 2001 the number of "repatriations" amounted to two million people (Karamanolis 2006:2).

According to the National Statistical Service of Greece (2004), 10 085 Africans were officially registered in Greece in 2004, Nigerians being the largest group (1022 persons, 730 men and 231 women), followed by Ghanaians (329 persons, 265 male and 58 female) (General Secretariat Of National Statistical Service Of Greece 2004). The number of illegal migrants however should be far higher. According to one of my informants, about 1000 Africans live in Thessaloniki alone. Her calculations were based on the sale of tickets for an African party that was nearly exclusively visited by Africans (Interview Kellie 04.10.04:1).

In relation to the illegal migrants, the number of people entering Greece legally is considerably lower. Precondition for entering is a green card and a residence permit, e.g. EU-citizens.

The number of applicants for political asylum is only about one to two percent of the complete foreign population, because the asylum procedure is complicated and only rarely successful. Most persons seeking political asylum receive neither financial nor social support (Lauth Bacas 2002:199f.).

Significant reasons for the high rate of immigration to Greece lie in the economic conditions of the countries of origin, in addition to political, religious or ethnic conflicts. On the other hand, the high immigration rate can also be explained by Greece's geographical position. The shoreline of altogether 15 000 km, the numerous islands and the long mountainous national borders are hard to protect against illegal immigration, particularly from Albania, via Turkey or from North Africa (Labrianidis, Lyberaki, Tinios, Hatziprokopiou 2004:1186; Fakiolas 2000:60). Social changes within Greece and the structure of the Greek labour market also promote immigration to the country. A large part of the Greek economy is based on little family businesses, whose production methods have a low technical standard and require a high quantum of low-qualified work. Since the majority of the Greeks have acquired a high educational standard, there is shortage of labour in simple and low-paid areas, which is met by flexible and cheap workers from abroad. As a rule, illegal occupation of foreign workers is quite popular not only because of low wages, but also because the national insurance contributions can be avoided under these circumstances. State controls of employment relations in small enterprises are still quite lenient (Fakiolas 2000:60ff.).

This applies particularly to domestic labour and the support of children and the elderly. Since Greek women have been entering the labour market with high qualifications and most Greek men still refuse to take on these traditionally female activities (Fakiolas 2000:60f.), the need for female migrants continuously increases. Meanwhile, nearly half of all immigrants in Greece are women supporting their families at home (Maratou-Alipranti, Fakiolas 2003:168). Although a considerable part of the migrants has passed through a higher education or obtained professional qualifications in their country of origin, in Greece they work in traditionally gender-specific and low-qualified jobs like farming, building and construction trade, or as domestic help, in the tourism industry or the entertainment and sex business. These jobs are not only badly respected, but also lacking social protection and are seasonally limited in many cases. The payment is considerably below the wage levels of Greeks, but sill far above the wages the migrants could earn in their countries of origin (Maratou-Alipranti, Fakiolas 2003:166, 175; Lauth Bacas 2002:203).

Meanwhile, a large proportion of the Greek economy depends on cheap labour supplied by migrants. In 1998 and 2001, the Greek government started regulation programmes, granting temporary legal status to many migrants who could prove a faultless certificate of conduct and a clean health certificate. Within these two years, about 370 000 migrants applied (Lauth Bacas 2002:200f.; Fakiolas 2000:74f.). Nonetheless, approximately one quarter of the migrants still lives and works in Greece without valid papers. Many illegal immigrants could not apply for the regulation programme because they had been previously convicted, were afraid of the police registration, were persuaded by their employers to continue illegal occupation or preferred the flexibility of this work themselves (Maratou-Alipranti, Fakiolas 2003:171). On the other hand new migrants enter the country who can not or do not want to legalize their status. Since the beginning of the 1990s migrants have been entering Greece by way of different networks, either through the help of family members or relatives in the country, or with the help of small Greek companies, which specifically recruit foreigners and promise them an occupation already before entry. By way of human trafficking numerous women and children are mediated into illegal prostitution (Fakiolas 2000:64f.).

## "African Thessaloniki": description of the field

The life of the African population in Thessaloniki is concentrated in two districts. In Evsonon in southern Thessaloniki, principally between the main streets Leoforos Stratou and Leoforos Vasilis, several businesses are located, serving as meeting places for Africans from this quarter or from the nearer surroundings. They include a gallery, a MoneyGram-Shop[21], two video-tape libraries and the bar "De Point", all run by Africans who hire African employees and -intential or not- have an almost exclusively African clientele. The video-libraries, which offer "Black Movies" and favourable telephone connections to the African

[21] Business chain for international transfer of funds

countries, serve Africans as a meeting place and for contacts to the respective native countries. In the bar "De Point" only African men, who lead a community life separate from women in some areas, met during the observation period.

The second "African" district extends from Odos Kassandrou up to Odos Phillipou. Several businesses, as well as telephone and internet stores are run by Africans here, as well as two Afro-Hairdressers, a Black-Streetwear-Shop and an African restaurant. Here and in Evsonon the African presence is more visible than in the other districts of the city, because many Africans use these businesses as locations of social exchange and assembly. The "Ebony Links Callcenter", in which an internet- and telephone shop is run by an African man and a hairdresser's salon by an African woman, also serves as a meeting place for many Africans of the surroundings to spend their free time and meet friends. One Afro-Hairdresser at Odos Kassandrou with mainly female customers, was not accessible to me because the owner declined to cooperate in my research.

Although the African restaurant "Mama Gee" is not as popular as the bar "De point" in Evsonon, it is nevertheless another centre of African life in Thessaloniki. Like the recently opened bar "Tadijo", the restaurant "Mama Gee" is one of the few facilities run by Africans which is used by both African and Greek visitors, although it lies in a side street and is only very hard to recognize because the sign still refers to the previous Greek possessors. The "Mama Gee's" inconspicuousness is no exception. African places usually are not recognizable as such immediately. An insider's knowledge is needed to find shops of African operators, because by their presentation they are not different from Greek stores. Only the bar "De Point" and the "Ebony Links Callcenter" are visible as African meeting places. At different times of the day a crowd of Africans sit on the street in front of these shops, especially in good weather and in the evening time.

The African bar "De Point" (Photo: Kathrin Leven)

## African migrant women: migration histories

Except for one, all women and men who have provided information during my field work came from Nigeria. The economic development of this country still suffers from the effects of corruption and military dictatorship ruling until 1999. A large portion of the population lives in poverty. Moreover, there are more than 400 different ethnic groups in Nigeria, while Muslim Hausa and Christian Yoruba and Ibo fight for supremacy in the country (Baratta 2000:581ff.). The economic problems and interethnic conflicts cause many Nigerians to leave their country for Europe. Greece serves as an admission gate rather than as a definite aim in Europe, although a large portion of the African migrants remains in the country in the end.

Although intercontinental migration from Africa to Europe is still dominated by men, a clear increase of female labour migration is visible particularly in Thessaloniki. In the following, I shall give a short introduction of biographical data and migration backgrounds of my main informants. To be able to keep the anonymity of the women, I have changed their names and used pseudonymes which the informants have chosen themselves for this purpose.

*Grace* is a 20 to 30-year-old Nigerian who has worked in one of the African video-libraries in Evsonon during the first weeks of my fieldwork. She is the oldest of four daughters of her mother. Her father had fifteen further women and altogether 57 children. Grace's father has died during her stay in Thessaloniki. At the time of his death he left four wives, among them also Grace's mother for whom she feels responsible as the oldest daughter. A part of her family lives in Africa today, two of her half-sisters live in Italy and earn their living as prostitutes. Grace has studied in her native country; however she had to break off the studies for financial reasons. First she had migrated to the Lebanon where she stayed for ten months without finding appropriate work. At this time, she met her Nigerian fiancé with whom she walked to Greece on foot via Syria and Turkey in 2000 (Interviews with Grace 16.09.04:1, 17.09.04:1, 18.09.04:2ff.).

I met eighteen-year-old *Mary* in the refugee accommodation in Thessaloniki. She was raised by her father until her 17th year of life, without having attended a school. Her

African Video Shop in the neighbouhood "Evsonon" (Photo: Kathrin Leven)

mother died when she was three years old, further family members do not exist. She and her father belonged to the Christian minority in the Muslim north of Nigeria. In the course of the civil war between the religious groups, her father was killed by Muslims while she escaped to Benin first, and further to Thessaloniki. On the ship to Greece, she got to know her present husband with whom she found shelter in the refugee accommodation in Thessaloniki after some days of homelessness. Because she does not speak any Greek and hoped for better labour opportunities being a native speaker of English, she tried to leave to Ireland illegally. She was intercepted at the Irish border and sent back to Greece where she spent a month in a Greek prison, and because of her fear of deportation to Nigeria attempted suicide (Interviews with Mary 30.09.04:1ff, 14.10.04:6f).

*Kellie* is 34 years old, from Lagos in the south of Nigeria. She passed through a thirteen years' school education and came to Greece as one of the first migrants in 1996. At first she lived in Athens before moving to Thessaloniki in 2000. She is unmarried and has a little daughter with whom she lives in an apartment in the district Evsonon. Since she has worked as a stripper in the past, she gave me most of my information about working conditions in the sex industry in Thessaloniki. Today Kellie runs the hairdresser store in the "Ebony Links Callcenter". Furthermore, she works as an independent hostess and appears as a stripper on private celebrations (Interview with Kellie 07.10.04:1ff.).

*Linda* is between 20 and 30 years old, from the west of Nigeria. Her father is a professor at a Nigerian university; she has studied music and dance in her native country. According to her statement, she had a good life in Nigeria, but wanted to finish her studies with a European examination. For this reason she also left her fiancé in Nigeria. Since she is in Thessaloniki, she finds no more time for studying though. Because of the lack of wellpaid jobs she has to spend all her time to earn her living (Interview with Linda 23.09.04:1).

*Clarice* is a 31 years old Nigerian with a degree as a children's nurse in Nigeria, who migrated to Kuwait after her graduation. There she became acquainted with her Nigerian husband George and followed him to Thessaloniki some years ago. They were planning to work together in Europe for some years and then to return to Africa to create a secure basis of livelihood for herself and her family. Georges came to Greece for studying 18 years ago. Since he did not get work after conclusion of his studies, he opened a store in the centre of Thessaloniki which he still runs today. Since one year Clarice and George also have been running the African restaurant "Mama Gee", to earn their living and to fund their return to Africa in the future (Interview with Clarice 06.10.04:1ff.).

Ebony Links Callcenter, with hairdresser´s shop (Photo: Kathrin Leven)

*Diana* is 32 years old and has been living in Thessaloniki for four years. She also followed her husband to Greece, who is thirteen years older than her and came to study in Thessaloniki fifteen years ago. After he left the university without degree because of the, in his opinion, racist structures, he opened a MoneyGram-Shop in the northern city centre which he and Diana operate together. Diana and her husband have two children who live with them in Thessaloniki. Although they live as a family in Greece, they are planning to return to Nigeria as soon as they have the according capital at their disposal (Interview with Diana 29.09.04:1).

*Jamilia* comes from Uganda and migrated to Greece to study. After completion of her five-year studies and an unsuccessful search for qualified work in Thessaloniki, she now is about to return to Uganda to find a work which corresponds to her abilities. In her opinion she is discriminated particularly as a black woman in Greece (Interview with Jamilia 04.10.04:1).

*Jane* has been in Thessaloniki since 2001. She is 36 years old, has one child and is married to an African man who is dependent on a kidney machine in a Greek hospital. The medical treatment is an essential reason for her stay in Greece for the time being (Group Interview 06.10.04).

*Farah* is 27 years old, from the south of Nigeria. She has been in Thessaloniki for two years and has a child. Farah's decision to migrate to Greece and to remain there is influenced substantially by the religious conflicts in her native country (Group Interview 06.10.04).

*Alithia* was born as a child of Nigerian immigrants in Thessaloniki. She is 19 years old, unmarried, does not have any children yet, lives with her parents and studies at the university of Thessaloniki (Group Interview 06.10.04).

## Reasons and aims of migration

Of the seven informants whose educational level is known to me, only Mary has no school education. Her departure to Europe was a flight from warlike disturbances. While Alithia, who was born in Thessaloniki, has also passed through her school education in Greece, five of my informants have obtained a higher school education in Africa. Some of them started to study or finished their studies already there; others have come to Europe for this purpose. The relatively high standard of education of female transnational migrants from Africa is confirmed by a study on the situation of African women in Vienna, which shows that 80% of the female African migrants have at least a middle school qualification, and almost 40% have completed their studies (Hamid 2003:26). Since these women have acquired comparatively high qualifications, a large part of them is not only searching for a well-paid job in Europe, but also for an employment in which their qualifications can be used and promoted. In Africa, women do not often find work that guarantees both good wages and high quality. More and more young women also come directly to Europe in order to study. They want to complete their studies with a western certificate, which is highly respected in Africa and guarantees an elevated professional position after their return (Koller 2003:59ff.). Furthermore, one of the most important aims in connection with the migration to Europe is the support of the family remaining in Africa and the construction of a secure basis of livelihood after returning.

Many of the women feel explicitly drawn to Europe by a deeply internalised picture of "Golden Europe" in the African societies. This picture is distributed and manifested particularly by the postcolonial educational systems, the media and by stories of former and present migrants. According to these representations, Europe is the continent of greener pastures, standing for material abundance everybody can profit from (Englert 1995:43ff.; Haferkamp 1989:109; Nsodu 2004:31ff.). From a distance, it is not realized that the European nations differ regarding their economic standards, economic problems and unemployment. Before migration, the European countries are seen as a unity which stands in a promising contrast to the impoverished African countries.

From all available sources and from my own interviews, it gets clear that this picture of Europe is maintained by all means even if the migrants have opposite experiences, because the relatives do not understand those as a reality, but as a personal failure. Newer examinations suggest that the families staying behind increasingly promote or even push the migration of women in particular, because a special loyalty of women to their relatives, and a higher reliability concerning the transfer of savings is assumed (Schöttes, Treibel 1997:103).

Most migrants do not aim at setting up durably or definitely in one of the European countries. The Africans rather plan to live in Europe only for some years, to save a lot of money during that time or to receive a good education and return to Africa to build up an economically, professionally and socially elevated existence there (Haferkamp 1989:93ff.). Especially women may also pursue further aims, such as transcending traditional gender roles, which can not be discussed within the scope of this article (Schöttes, Treibel 1997:86f.).

## Wage labour

It seems to be a forlorn hope for the African migrant women in Thessaloniki to find work that is legal and well paid at the same time. Legal work which can be obtained with a green card is usually time consuming and badly paid. Working as a domestic help in a Greek family household is such a job, the monthly wage ranging between 500 and 600 Euro. Frequently, the housekeepers take over further tasks like cooking and child-caring without any financial compensation. Moreover, two informants report that agreements reached at the beginning of the contract are often not observed, particularly regarding contributions to health insurance. This means that the women can even get problems with the prolongation of their visa, because they have not met their liability to pay tax and health insurance contributions (Interviews with Grace 17.09.04:1f.; Kellie 04.10.04:1).

The work in Greek factories was described as similarly problematic. For working seven days a week, the monthly salary amounts to 600 Euro. Also in factories, it happens that the payment is either delayed or too low. Grace, who has worked in a town near Thessaloniki, describes that she had worked 31 days in a month and done additional hours of overtime, which should be paid with three Euro per hour. Contrary to the agreement to be paid weekly, she was paid only 150 Euro at the end of the month altogether (Interview with Grace 18.09.04:4).

## Self-employment

Grace's experiences coincide with the statements of Linda, who is now self-employed and sells perfume in the surrounding villages of Thessaloniki, because she grew tired of not being paid or being dismissed by Greek employers again and again (Interview with Linda 23.09.04:1). This form of self-employment is a way out of the largely unsatisfactory Greek labour market, frequently chosen by African migrants. Like Mary, many women go to the villages and sell electronic equipment, children's toys and jewellery. They drive with their own or a borrowed car, or go by bus, either alone or in a group. There they walk from one restaurant to the next and offer their goods. As a rule, the women have a license for this work which, however, does not permit them to sell their goods in the streets of Thessaloniki or on a market (Group Interview 06.10.04:1ff.). Selling goods in the streets of Thessaloniki is illegal, but is nonetheless operated mostly by African men who offer CDs, DVDs or posters, permanently watching out for the police. Selling on the market in Thessaloniki seems to be a typical activity for African women who are married to another African in Greece (Interview with Diana 29.09.04:1). I do not know if it is easier for married women to get a license for a market stand, or whether they pursue this activity illegally, which seems improbable to me because they would possibly risk expulsion and therefore the separation from their families.

Another form of self-employment is opening a business of one's own. This presupposes financial possibilities and furthermore contains a certain risk because a visa in Greece is not automatically prolonged, just because a migrant has built up his own business in the country. So it is theoretically possible to be expelled despite a store of one's own and to suffer big financial losses this way (Interview with Clarice 06.10.04:3). However, a storekeeper I interviewed did not assess this risk too highly, because according to him the Greek government leaves African store owners alone, as long as they pay their taxes and do not violate the law (Interview in the video library 11.10.04:TB). The majority of the Africans sell various household effects, little electrical appliances and African products in their own business, or offer miscellaneous services, for example computer processing and photocopies, foreign transfers and telephone connections abroad.

Bars run by Africans are a relatively recent phenomenon. In the course of the last year, the bar "De point" in Evsonon and the "Tadijo" in the city centre were opened. According to my observations, most businesses have been built up by men and are run either by them alone or together with their wives who followed later. Only in one case known to me, a married couple has opened a business, the restaurant "Mama Gee", together. The more and more frequent decision of migrants to be self-employed has also been registered in the scientific literature and by the local Greek authorities (Fakiolas 2000:65). However, it remains unclear why women go into self-employment by selling things far from the city with a vendor's tray, instead of building up a store of their own in the city like the men do. A possible explanation is that the African men in Thessaloniki are linked through a closer network than the African women and possibly award a start-up capital among each other. Another explanation would be the generally higher status of men in the Greek society, which might cause higher salaries in traditionally male fields of work so that they have more equity capital at their disposal than the female migrants. This assumption is supported by numerous studies showing that that women are not only put at a disadvantage due to their migrant status, but also due to their gender (Tastsoglou, Hadjicostandi 2003:197f.).

If women run a business of their own, it usually is a hairdresser store offering Afro hairstyles, which appeal primarily to female African customers. Sometimes the women run their business alone, or they share the store area with other Africans. Kellie runs her hairdresser's salon in a back room of the "Ebony Links Callcenter" without being married or in a relation to the African operator. But the earnings by hairdressing are no longer high since the beginning of the 1990s. At this time the migration of female Africans to Greece increased, who were then pressing into the hairdresser business and increasing competition (Interview with Kellie 07.10.04:1). The long working hours and bad income in legal jobs are reasons for many African women to look for fast and large money in the sex industry. Kellie, who changed from the hairdresser to the striptease business herself, also describes:

> „There is no job in Greece, no job. They [the African women, remark of the author] are fed up with this rubbish, [...] because they say the decent job is too cheap. Like for example they go to cleaning, they have to work and work from morning till the next, the next day till the morning and only to get 600 Euros. And this 600 Euros, you can get it in three days." (Interview with Kellie 07.10.04:6)

## Sex work in Greece

The term "sex work" refers to various forms of sexual services including striptease, telephone sex, pornography or service in an animation-restaurant, although these activities do not compulsorily include prostitution. Especially NGOs working with the concept of sex work point out that prostitution is only one of various forms of sexual service. Regarding sexual exploitation, also all other forms have to be taken seriously. The boundaries between sex work excluding and including prostitution are often fluent, when women cannot make a living in the labour market. All forms of sex work, particularly striptease in nightclubs and erotic animation in ordinary bars, can be found in Thessaloniki, even in the exclusive commercial centre of the city.

No exact data exist on the number of female migrants working in the Greek sex industry. At a conference on "Trafficking in Women"[22] in Athens in 2003, female illegal migrants forced into the prostitution in Greece were estimated at about 20 000 (BBC News 2001: Greek sex industry uncovered). On the other hand, the number of women who only find work in the sex industry due to the restricted labour market, or who have migrated deliberately to earn money by sex work is far higher. The women who work as prostitutes meet a high demand in Greece. More than one million Greeks use the sexual services of prostitutes (BBC News 2001: Greek sex industry uncovered). With a total population of about 10.3 million inhabitants, this means that approximately every second male Greek in the sexually mature age has his sexual claims satisfied by prostitutes.

This high rate can be explained by a traditional gender stereotype, which still stamps the social understanding of male and female sexuality, despite recent emancipation movements in Greece. According to this traditional position, strong sexual drives are inherent in men, which make them naturally different from women. Male sexual activity before, respectively outside of marriage, is justified by this difference (Loizos, Papataxiarchis 1991:222). For this reason, prostitution is regarded in Greece as a necessary evil to satisfy the needs of the men, which a decent woman or wife may not satisfy. Besides masturbation, visiting a prostitute is therefore a generally accepted outlet for the assumed irrepressible male drives. For men who call on the service of the prostitute, no negative stigmatization exists. Women who prostitute themselves are still excluded vehemently from society, because their sexual behaviour completely contradicts the female role ideal and they are considered dangerous and dirty (Lazaridis 2001: 74ff.; Meyer 1994:69ff.).

[22] "Trafficking in women" was defined by the UN in 1994 as "the illicit and clandestine movement of persons across national and international border with the end goal of forcing women and girl children into sexually or economically oppressive situations for the profit of recruiters, traffickers and crime syndicates, as well as other illegal activities related to trafficking, such as forced domestic labour, false marriages, clandestine employment and false adoption" (Wijers and Lap-Chew 1997:22, quotes after Lazaridis 2001:68f).

The Greek state does not explicitly prohibit prostitution, but tries to keep it under control and away from public view. Accordingly, prostitutes should be registered and work only in registered brothels, as well as undergoing regular health controls. According to a law of 1981 for "protection against sexually transferable diseases", women can register as prostitutes when they are at least 21 years old, unmarried or divorced and of Greek nationality. With the registration as prostitutes, the women exclude themselves from Greek society, but they risk imprisonment for up to three years if they work illegally. In practice, arrests and prison sentences of more than a year are rare. However, the number of female migrants arrested in connection with prostitution by far surpasses that of the Greek women, because the migrants do not possess the papers which allow them to prostitute (Lazaridis 2001:76f).

## Migrants in the sex industry

Kellie came to Greece in 1996 and worked in Athens in a hairdresser's salon after her arrival. When her earnings got lower due to increasing competition and she could not send sufficient money to Africa any longer, she started to dance in a striptease bar. According to her information, in 1999 no Africans worked in this business, but mainly British, German, Dutch and Norwegian women. She earned a lot of money in a short time and arranged for other African women to work in the striptease-bars who again arranged jobs for their female friends (Interview with Kellie 07.10.04:1).

Still today and with a certain pride, she points out that she has discovered and established this branch of profession for Africans. Although she got out about three years ago, she says that she is still known to every African of this business and is treated obligingly in every striptease bar (Interview with Kellie 07.10.04:5f.). This pride is based on her opinion, that the job as a striptease dancer was of a higher quality at her active times but has lost this today. There was, according to her, a strict agreement between the women about what is part of the striptease job. Besides dancing, the job consisted only in conversation with the male visitors while the men treated them to drinks and therefore increased the sales volume of the bar. Being touched by the visitors or prostitution was strictly forbidden. These regulations were supported by the women's Green card, which legalized the work as a stripper but prohibited work as prostitutes (Interview with Kellie 07.10.04:3).

Today the job is spoiled, according to Kellie's view. She blames the Russian migrant women for this development by trying to earn as much money as possible without holding on to any rules (Interview with Kellie 07.10.04:3). According to Kellie's assessment, the formerly strict separation between striptease and prostitution has dissolved completely within the last few years. The women still dance, but try to snatch the customers away from each other to spend a well-paid night with them when they are not on stage. A real fight for the favour of rich visitors has broken out in those bars where the women try to outbid each other by indecency (Interview with Kellie 07.10.04:5). Women who can not or do not want to get out of this business are forced to carry this development:

> *„The woman will stand up to go and make her dance on stage. Another girl comes who wants to do what she didn't do to him, like taking the customers hand, put it in the pussy and making all this rubbish. Then the customer like her doing this to him. So this is what causes the problem."* (ibid.)

This unconditional rush for profit not only ruins the income in the business but also strongly endangers the health of the women. Moreover, the women are at risk because the police are aware of this development and send officials to the bars who pass themselves off as customers and arrest the women when they agree to prostitution. The sentence for this form of illegal prostitution is on average three months in prison, after which the women are discharged and in most cases may remain in Greece (Interview with Kellie 07.10.04:3).

My internal knowledge of the development in the striptease bars and the situation of the Africans was conveyed exclusively by Kellie, since none of the other informants had worked as a stripper. However, most of the African women I interviewed also have a more or less comprehensive knowledge about the occupation of female African migrants in the striptease bars. Although Mary had never worked in the sex industry herself, she told me that many African women work in striptease bars and, as she expressed it, put up with everything. She had met an African woman in prison who was arrested because she prostituted herself in the described way (Interview with Mary 14.10.04:6). Also Grace knew that African women not only work in the striptease bars of Thessaloniki but also in the rural surroundings and not only dance there but also sleep with the customers (Interview with Grace 24.09.04:8). This phenomenon was also to referred by African men. During one evening in the "Rasta Club", one of the reggae bars in Thessaloniki, I asked a male informant why no African women were present. He answered with a characteristic smile, that African women would come here in the early morning, because they had to finish work first. Not only the operators of the striptease bars, but also ordinary bar owners profit from the difficulties of African migrants on the legal Greek labour market. According to Kellie's description, African women are hired there also to lure male customers:

> *„They don't work in the back of the bar, they work outside the bar. Customers come, they play with them, the customers buy drinks for them. [...]The girls they make drinks like that. And they make a lot of drinks, more than those working in the strip club. [...] And we have a lot of them in a lot of bars in Thessaloniki. We have each one over than five girls, the least is four girls."* (Interview with Kellie 07.10.04:6)

I cannot judge how many barkeepers use the stereotype of the exotic and sexually attractive African in this way, but I have experienced an evening in the bar "Tadijo", where an African woman was sitting at the end of the counter who on the day before had been working in the service. A white visitor permanently sought body contact with her, put his hands on her hips, hugged her and tried to kiss her. Her reactions suggested that she was an erotic hostess, since she stayed close to him all the time and allowed him to touch her but did not touch him herself and fended off the attempted kiss. Kellie reports that many Africans meanwhile leave the striptease job, due to its degrading working conditions and work in this way in the ordinary bars. But in her opinion, these fields of activity are not fundamentally different. Also in the ordinary bars, the women have to suggest sexual availability to assert themselves against their competitors and legitimise their employment by particularly high earnings for the barkeeper. Presumably also in these cases the women themselves can only earn higher amounts when they agree to further-reaching sexual actions with the customers and spend the night with them. Also the African woman described before left the "Tadijo bar" together with her admirer, despite her obvious reluctance.

In contrast, Kellie has discovered a form of self-employment for herself which guarantees the separation between show and prostitution and which is largely unknown among Africans in this form. Today, she performs show programs on private parties that involve striptease-dancing but no further sexual activity. Obviously, she has achieved sufficient publicity by the distribution of her calling card and by word of mouth, to be financially successful in this job by now (Interview with Kellie 07.10.04:2).

Ordinary prostitution does not happen in the centre of Thessaloniki, but in the comparatively shabby quarter of Vardaris, in the southeast of the city. According to Kellie, the foreign women who work here are in possession of a green card which authorizes them to work as prostitutes for three years. African prostitutes are not visible in the street, though.

I am not able to exclude with certainty if some prostitution in Vardaris is coercive, with the women being kept in apartments and their suitors being arranged by a pimp. The Green Card mentioned by Kellie and the official registration of the women is an argument against this theory. According to an employee of the „Rehabilitation Centre of Torture and other Forms of Abuse“, no trafficking victim from Africa was notified until today to this Non Government Organization, but she regards it as possible that the police turns its attention towards the East European women and therefore does not recognize African coercive prostitutes as such (Interview with CRTV 17.09.04:1).

## Migration routes to Thessaloniki

Most Africans do not think that African women are forced into the sex-industry or into prostitution (Interviews with Kellie 07.10.04:4; Laurence 30.09.04: TB). At closer analysis of the migration ways from African women to Greece, parallels to trafficking of women become obvious, however. Regarding the lack of alternatives for African women on the Greek labour market, a suggestive compulsion to sex work must be stated after all. It was Kellie again who imparted the knowledge about the beginnings and the development of the migration of African women to Greece.

When she came to Greece in 1996, the share of the African population was still so small that she had to spend a week in the streets until she met the first African. That man helped her to take the first steps for her long-term stay in the country (Interview with Kellie 04.10.04:1). By now, a system has established within the African community by which compatriots are helped into Greece. Those who already have a legal status and an established existence in Greece pay for the plane tickets, organize the necessary papers for the legal stay in the country and search for an occupation for the newcomers (Interview with Kellie 07.10.04:1f.). Like Kellie, their expenditures and efforts are paid well and they open up new opportunities for themselves to earn money besides their regular job. This kind of support for compatriots is thus not based on an explicit solidarity between Africans, but rather on the possibility of earning a lot of money with relatively small effort – sums between 2000 and 6000 Euro were mentioned.

There is no guarantee that help given will be actually paid for, however. In Kellie's case, one African woman whom she had helped to Thessaloniki had not paid until the time of my fieldwork. Of course there is no legal form of pressure to force those persons to pay, because apparently written contracts are not used in these private agreements. Besides, the resulting claims would hardly be compatible with Greek legislation. Kellie has definitely adjusted her participation in such transactions after this last experience. Only in family affairs she still makes an exception and at present tries to get her brother into the country. In this case, she is presumably willing to invest her own money even without repayment (Interview with Kellie 15.10.04:7f.).

However, this system is not only occasionally misused by migrants entering the country, but increasingly by those who offer to help. While in the beginning, the usual charge about tripled their own expenses, helpers today sometimes take more than tenfold of their own expenditure. So an African woman in some cases has debts of up to 50 000 Euro when entering the country, which she has to pay off as fast as possible. At this point there remains hardly any alternative to sex work and prostitution. Sometimes these women help further African women into the country when they have paid off their own debts, and let them pay a similar amount, leading to a circle of abuse (Interviews with Kellie 07.10.04:7, Grace 24.09.04:8). According to Kellie however, some of the heavily mortgaged women who do not want to work in prostitution also go to the police.

Obviously this system can be dangerous to women who do not pay off their debts and to their families, since many of them have signed contracts before their entry that grant their parents´ land to the contractors, if the daughter does not pay within a year (Interviews with Kellie 15.10.04:8, Grace 24.09.04:8). At this point, the parallels to trafficking in women become quite obvious. Even if the African women are not held as prisoners or are forced to prostitution by physical means, many of them do not have any other choice than prostitution. Different from coercive prostitution though is that the women still are in possession of their visa. Even though they are not officially allowed to prostitute, they can move freely at least. Theoretically, they have the possibility to decide for themselves and live freely after payment of all debts; while coercive prostitutes never have a realistic chance at any time. However, since the women are often arrested and expelled because of illegal prostitution they have to be smuggled into Greece once more to pay off their old debts, and in this way make new debts again. Grace pointed out an African woman to me who had to pay off 80 000 Euro exactly for this reason (Interview with Grace 24.09.04:8).

Both Grace and Mary report that tractor activities are not organized only by Greeks, but also by Africans who visit families and offer a supposedly good job in Europe for the daughter. If the family agrees, contracts are concluded about the repayment of the debts and the women often only notice when they are in Europe, that they are to work in prostitution or have no other choice to settle their debts. In some cases the women know that they will go into prostitution in Europe, but can not assess the circumstances in which they have to work (Interviews with Grace 24.09.04:8, Mary 14.10.04:6). As in other migrant groups (cf. Fakiolas 2000:64f.), since the end of the 1990s networks have established in the African population in Thessaloniki, which facilitate the reuniting of further compatriots. These supports are differently motivated and the reasons range from a desire for reuniting families to criminal human trafficking. Africans who were smuggled into the country themselves and help other Africans into Greece after their entry to be able to pay off their own debts, take an intermediate position in these processes. In these cases, the women were victims of the system themselves at times, but cause a vicious circle to improve their own situation.

## Supporting the family

The limitations of the regular Greek labour market frustrate the common goal of earning a lot of money in only a few years and returning to Africa to build up a better existence for the family there. The return to Africa moves even further because of the debts raised for the entry, the lack of capital for the construction of a better existence in Africa and the expectations of the family remaining there, who would be disappointed at an unsuccessful return and possibly would get impoverished. Due to the low income of the migrants, the financial support of the family can only be managed with difficulties even while they are in Europe. In most cases, the journey to Europe was financed by the extended family and a circle of friends who therefore have great expectations towards the migrants. They need money for the maintenance of their houses, medical supply and particularly for the school education of their children in Africa, which enormously enlarges the pressure to meet these liabilities at all costs (McIntyre 2004:135f.).

The migrants´ burden is made even greater by the African stereotypes about Europe. Relatives remaining there can not imagine that life in Europe could be fraught with financial difficulties. Besides the rent for an apartment and possibly for business premises in Thessaloniki, besides the taxes, health insurance and the costs of daily life and the care of the children or the husband, hardly anything is left to send to the family in Africa. Grace supports her mother in Nigeria: With an income of 400 Euro in the video library and the money which her friend earns by selling CDs, just enough money remains for renting the apartment at 250 Euro and the daily cost of living. Because of the lack of financial reserves, she even cannot help her family in emergency cases. When her father died last year, she could not travel to Africa, which was hard to explain to her relatives (Interview with Grace 18.08.04:5).

Clarice and her husband had invested their available money into the "Mama Gee" and were still highly indebted at the time of the research. Nonetheless the support of their family in Africa had topmost priority, so they had only five hours left to sleep after daily work and the care of their children (Interview with Clarice 06.06.04:1).

Mary who does not have to support any family members in Africa, is dependent on support herself. She lives in an apartment which costs 180 Euro together with her husband and a mutual friend. Her husband earns 200 to 400 Euro monthly by his work in a factory, which must suffice for the life of the partners since Mary only occasionally looks after the children of African couples and in this way irregularly contributes to the income (Interview with Mary 14.10.04:6).

Only Kellie had at least at times earned very well by the striptease job and her migration organization. Also today, obviously she has a good income as a hairdresser and a hostess. At the time of the research she had recently returned from a journey to Africa and was also helping her brother into Europe at her own expense. She is therefore one of the few Africans who could at least partially put her migration aims into effect and even started a chain migration (Interview with Kellie 15.10.04:8).

## Conclusion

As the previous sections have shown, African women have been migrating to Greece since the middle of the 1990s, in search of opportunities for earning money and securing a better life in Africa. The number of the Africans in Thessaloniki is growing steadily, since Greece is supposed to serve as an admission gate into Europe, but many migrants remain in the country. Migration is motivated by idealistic ideas of Europe, which are usually disappointed.

Since more demanding professional activities are limited to Greek men and recently also to Greek women, the African women must take on unqualified work. In these areas they are not able to use or improve the education and qualifications they had obtained in their native country or even in Greece. They frequently work in traditionally gender-specific areas in which they are paid worse than their male compatriots. For this reason, they rarely manage to build up an existence of their own, independent of the discriminatory Greek labour market. African women are only self-employed in low-qualified areas or together with their husbands.

The entertainment and sex business offers a potential labour market for African women in Thessaloniki. By the lack of alternatives, but also by transnational networks similar to woman trafficking, African women are not only increasingly driven into different areas of the sex industry, but especially into illegal prostitution.

In the end, most African migrants remain much longer in Greece than actually planned and are also not able to support their relatives in Africa as comfortably as expected before their entry.

# Strategies of Transnationalism: Albanian Migrant Women in Thessaloniki

Elke Haas

Since the early 1990s, an increasing trend of migrants developing and maintaining social networks between the countries of residence and of origin has been discussed in the context of ´transnationalism` (Glick Schiller, Basch, Blanc-Szanton 1992: ix,1). In this paper, which is based on my fieldwork, I shall examine transnationalism of Albanian migrant women in Thessaloniki. Further questions relate to the factors promoting transnationalism, and to its practice in everyday life.

After placing the term ´transnationalism` in a theoretical context, I shall give some general background information on Albania and Albanian migration. The collapse of the communist regime in 1991 led to instable political and economic conditions causing massive emigration from Albania to neighbouring countries. During the last decades, Greece has experienced a transformation from an emigration to an immigration country. It has become the main destination of the recent Albanian migration (Mai, Schwandner-Sievers 2003: 941). The Albanian women in my study have left Albania since the early 1990s, due to a lack of short-term perspectives. Their migratory goal is a "better" life after returning to Albania.

Albanian social networks in Thessaloniki, especially Albanian associations serve a dual function for the migrants, both facilitating daily life in the country of residence (job search and social contacts), and maintaining contact to Albania and Albanian culture. The identification of migrants with Albania is strengthened by Albanian language courses, Albanian newspapers and the celebration of Albanian holidays. Thus, practicing transnationalism is the key factor for maintaining the migrant women's connection to their homeland. Implementing transnationalism includes routine border-crossing, communication, as well as remittances to family members in Albania. Transnationalism guarantees the possibility of returning home. As demonstrated by Labrianidis and Hatziprokopiou these relationships persist after their return (Labrianidis, Hatziprokopiou 2005:114f.).

## Theoretical framework: the concept of ´transnationalism`

According to Mai and Schwandner-Sievers, Albanian migration in the 1990s is an essentially transnational socio-cultural phenomenon, not only caused by the post-communist conditions in Albania, but also by the political and economic conditions in the neighbouring countries Greece and Italy (Mai, Schwandner-Sievers 2003:939). They consider transnationalism as:

> "one of the founding dimensions of current globalising trends, referring to the emergence of new socio-cultural, political and economic interconnections between sub-national and supra-national spaces and actors as a consequence of the loss of power at a national level" (Mai, Schwandner-Sievers 2003:947).

In the early 1990s, research increasingly focused on immigrants building cross-border contacts to their home, even when the countries of origin and of residence are separated by great distances:

> "the process by which immigrants build social fields that link together their country of origin and of settlement" (Glick Schiller, Basch, Blanc-Szanton 1992:1).

Immigrants that develop cross-border networks have been labelled ´transmigrants`:

> "Transmigrants develop and maintain multiple relations – familial, economic, social, organizational, religious, and political that span borders. Transmigrants take actions, make decisions, and feel concerns, and develop identities within social networks that connect them to two or more societies simultaneously" (ibid.:1f.).

Through these cross-border networks they are integrated in two or more cultures and countries. Transmigrants often pursue economic, social and political interest (ibid.:1f.; Phizacklea 2003:79f.; Westwood, Phizacklea 2000:2,10). The connotation ´transnational` in contrast to ´international` stresses multinational, permanent relationships and regular movements over national borders by individuals and organisations, rather than by states or nations (Kokot 2004:9; Kokot, Tölölyan, Alfonso 2004:4). Phizacklea defines ´transnational` as:

> "the many and varied transactions and processes that migrants maintain between ´home` (as in ´where I was born`) and ´home` (where I am now)" (Phizacklea 2003:81).

Accordingly, migrants´ transactions are not necessarily limited to business-issues, but can include simpler forms like buying a telephone card to call the family at home, celebrating family events or preserving certain cultural symbols like dances, food and religious practices. This transnationalism in daily life has been called ´transnationalism from below` (Levitt 2001:6; Phizacklea 2003:80f.).

Practicing transnationalism can be facilitated by geographical factors. This is the case for Albanian migration, where the proximity of Greece and Italy to Albania and the access to transport routes ease the practice of transnationalism. The economic factor is crucial. Since the migratory decision was often made in order to improve the economic situation of the whole family, migrants keep visiting and supporting their family in Albania, maintaining constant cross-borders flows of people, goods and money (Barbaja, King 2005:1, 20f.; Labrianidis, Hatziprokopiou 2005:95, 113; Fakiolas 2000:64; Mai, Schwandner-Sievers 2003:939) The transnational character of the current Albanian migration results from a combination of family networks and responsibilities, as well as geographic facilitation (Barjaba, King 2005:20, Labrianidis, Hatziprokopiou 2005:113f.). Thus, according to Labrianidis and Hatziprokopiou:

> "many Albanians, especially who went to Greece, manage to live effectively *between* two countries, either by coming and going for temporary work, or by organising their lives in both places of origin an destination, with the latter providing the material resources for the acquisition of income and the improvement of the ´home` conditions" (ibid.:95).

## Albanian migration to Greece

Migration from Albania began in the early 1990s, caused by the collapse of the communist regime which had ruled since 1944 and by the ensuing political and economic instability. Despite democratic elections, chaotic political conditions dominated by nepotism, corruption and financial scandals, thrust Albania into political and economic instability (Barjaba, King 2005:3, Gashi, Steiner 1997:268ff.).

Many Albanians who had migrated to Greece returned to Albania until 1995. In 1997 however, the breakdown of the so called pyramid system[23] caused financial ruin of a great deal of the population and led to a second massive wave of emigration, especially to Greece and Italy. Albanian migration is continuing to this day (Karakatsanis, Swarts 2003:240; Labrianidis, Lyberaki, Tinios, Hatziprokopiou 2004:1183ff.; Fakiolas 2000:57ff., 70; Lazaridis, Psimenos 2000:175f.).

A short look at the conditions during the communist period will show the multiple factors involved in Albanian migration. After the communist party came to power under Enver Hoxha in 1944, all borders were closed. During the following 45 years Albania was isolated from the rest of the world. In 1948, Albania broke its close political and economic relations to Yugoslavia and became an ally of the Soviet Union. In February 1961, Hoxha negotiated an economic treaty with China. In December of the same year, relations with the Soviet Union were terminated. In 1967 religion was forbidden. Up to this time the majority of Albanians had been Muslim. In 1978, relations with China broke down. Hoxha`s rule ended with his death in 1985, his successor was Ramiz Alia (Gashi, Steiner 1997:268ff.).

Under Hoxha`s regime, all movements were centrally coordinated and controlled. Internal migration was severely limited. External migration was completely forbidden. Even today, many Albanians consider this restriction of mobility as the greatest limitation of their personal freedom during communist rule. During Hoxha`s regime, telephone and postal services were monitored. To protect the borders from "foreign invasion", the coun-

[23] Since 1992, certain investment companies, supported by the government, offered investments with very high interest-rates.

try was covered with countless bomb shelters. Roads were left in disrepair in order to make it more difficult for an enemy to conquer the country. Albania was propagated as a "workers´s paradise". In contrast, the West was chastised for its decadence and immorality (Kressing 2002:11f.; Mai 2002:42ff.; Pichler 2002:133f.).

Foreign, especially Italian television, viewed with illegal satellite receivers, was the only source of information from abroad. The presentation of beauty, wealth and entertainment in Italian television led to the illusion that all this could be achieved in the West without the investment of effort. Combined with the experience of limited mobility, this notion became the driving force of many migratory projects (Mai 2005:543ff.). Thus, for many migrants, emigration meant not only covering a geographic distance, but prevailing over the communist past:

> "In this respect Albanians, migrating a few tens of kilometres across the sea to Italy or over the mountains to Greece, were making the longest journey: out of their history. Their short migration paths similar landscapes and climates, but bridged the chasm from an ideologised, collectivised past that was collapsing all around them to a utopian mythologised West which for them [...] was seen as a land of leisure and plenty, glimpsed mainly through the clandestine watching of Italian television" (Barjaba, King 2005:6).

## Greece as a destination for migrants

Until the 1970es, Greece had been a country of emigration. More than ten percent of the Greek population, almost one million people, emigrated after the post-war period, mainly to Western Europe, Australia and North America. During the 1970es, many Greeks returned to their homeland. Today the number of emigrating Greeks is very low. Since the 1980es, Greece has become a destination for migrants from Eastern Europe and Third World countries

In this context, female immigration to Greece should be taken into particular consideration. Within Europe, Greece has the highest rate of female immigration. At the end of the

20th century, 60% of all migrants were women[24] (Droukas 1998:348; Karakatsanis, Swarts 2003:240; Labrianidis, Lyberaki, Tinios, Hatziprokopiou 2004:1183ff.; Fakiolas 2000:57ff., 70; Lazaridis, Psimenos 2000:175f.).

Geographic, economic and political factors make Greece an attractive goal for international migration. Greece's long coast line, numerous islands and mountainous borders make illegal entry relatively easy (Anthias, Lazaridis 2000:3). Most Albanian migrants enter Greece across the mountainous border. For Albanian immigration, the geographic proximity of country of origin and residence is a crucial factor in their migratory decision, facilitating the maintenance of contacts to their home country (Tastsoglou, Hadjicostanti 2003:195), and determining the transnational character of Albanian migration (Labrianidis, Hatziprokopiou 2005:95).

Political developments in Greece such as the integration into the European Union, increasing political stability and a functioning welfare system also contribute to the increase in immigration. (Agelopoulos 2000:147ff.; Droukas 1998:350; Labrianidis, Lyberaki, Tinios, Hatziprokopiou 2004:1187f.; Fakiolas 2000:60; Lazaridis, Psimenos 2000:175). Current regularisation programmes of illegal immigration are also conducive to immigration. In the beginning of the immigration period until the end of 1997, the Greek government had followed a very restrictive immigration policy and reacted to illegal immigration with repressive methods. Between 1991 and 1995, approximately one million Albanian immigrants were deported. Due to this policy, many illegal Albanian immigrants remained without a residence and work permit (Barjaba, King 2005:10ff.; Fakiolas 2000:61, 72f.; Lazaridis, Psimenos 2000:175). In January of 1998, the Greek government liberalised its immigration policy and instituted a programme to legalise illegal migrants.[25]

[24] 70% of Albanian and 80% of the Philippine migrants

[25] This programme allowed immigrants to obtain the *White Card,* those with a regular income could obtain the *Green Card*. Both guaranty the same social benefits to immigrants as to Greek citizens. The *Type A Green Card* is valid for a duration of one to three years (depending on the labour market), *Type B* for five years. Until May 1999, 65% of 371 641 applicants for the *White Card* were Albanians. During the second regularisation programme of 2001, 231 996 migrants applied for the *Green Card*. Migrants of Greek ethnic origin, i.e. the Greek minority of Southern Albania, were given a special legal status. Upon proof of their Greek origin, they receive a special card for ethnic Greeks (*homogeni card*) (Barjaba and King 2005: 12, Fakiolas 2000: 72ff., Hatziprokopiou 2003: 1036f., Lauth Bacas 2002: 2000f., Mai and Schwandner-Sievers 2003: 941).

Declining birth rates and the ensuing aging of the population have led to changes in the Greek labour market, resulting in demand for unqualified and low qualified labour. Due to their high educational level, a large sector of the Greek work force is not willing to accept a job below their level of qualification. Greece's many small and middle-sized enterprises with labour intensive production require inexpensive workers with low qualifications. This imbalance of supply and demand in the Greek labour market is compensated by migrant workers, who must be more flexible relating to wages and working conditions. They work for wages below the Greek standard, but above those at home. Male Albanian migrants work mostly in the building sector or in agriculture. Albanian women find work in the domestic sector. As in the rest of the world, the demand for domestic servants has increased drastically in Greece since the 1980s (Anthias, Lazaridis 2000:5; Labrianidis, Lyberaki, Tinios, Hatziprokopiou 2004:1195f.; Fakiolas 2000:60f.; Lazaridis, Psimenos 2000:173f., 180).

There are few reliable data on the number of Albanian migrants in Greece or Thessaloniki, since the proportion of undocumented migrants is unknown. The Albanian Ministry of Labour and Social Affairs estimates the number of post-communist migrants at 800 000: 500 000 of them reside in Greece. This is about one fourth of the population of Albania at the beginning of the twenty-first century. Almost any Albanian family is confronted by migration (Barjaba, King 2005:10; Fakiolas 2000:57; Gjonça 2002:16; Kaser, Pichler, Schwandner-Sievers 2002:8; Karakatsanis, Swarts 2003:240f.; Labrianidis, Hatziprokopiou 2005:97; Mai, Schwandner-Sievers 2003:941).

According to another estimation by the Greek government in 1999, 65% of the total 371 641 applicants for regularisation were Albanians. Including those who did not apply for regularisation, the number of Albanian migrants in Greece could be estimated at about half a million (Labrianidis, Lyberaki, Tinios, Hatziprokopiou 2004:1189ff.; Lazaridis, Psimenos 2000:17; Karakatsanis, Swarts 2003:240; Lauth Bacas 2002: 2004). In Thessaloniki, the unofficial number of Albanian migrants is about 50 000, whereas in 1998, the number of Albanian applicants in Thessaloniki was 19 807 (Hatziprokopiou 2003:1055).

## Albanian women in Thessaloniki: goals and motivations

During my fieldwork, I interviewed thirteen women from Albania, who had come to Thessaloniki between 1990 and 2002. Most contacts were made through Albanian associations in Thessaloniki. Except for one woman, who was able to speak English, the interviews were conducted in Greek which is neither their mother language nor mine. Two of the women whom I met several times invited me to their home and introduced me to their families. They asked me to visit them again, should I ever come back to Thessaloniki.

Most women had migrated with their husbands and children (cf. also Cavounidis 2003: 229, 231, 237). Some of the women had entered Greece alone and their families joined them later on. Parents and other family members relatively often also live in Greece. About a third of the women had left Albania before 1995, one in 1990. From 1997 to 1998, after the collapse of the pyramid system, a further third of them had emigrated. The others migrated to Thessaloniki between 1999 and 2002. All had emigrated due to the instable economic and political conditions in post-communist Albania.

According to a survey in *Albanian Human Development Report* 2000 (UNDP 2000), economic and other living conditions were the main motivation for Albanian emigration. The relatively low income in Albania in comparison to the European average and the high unemployment rate are not the only key factors. The rapid deterioration of the economic, political and social situation is also crucial. Between 1991 and 1993 unemployment rose from 9% to 29%, a threefold increase within two years (Barjaba, King 2005:21).

The women in my study shared these reasons for migration. The lack of perspectives in Albania led them to go abroad. Their motivation was mainly economic, since rising unemployment made it impossible for them to sustain themselves. Therefore, the question of wages for their labour dominates their daily life (Lazaridis 2000: 63ff.; Labrianidis, Lyberaki, Tinios, Hatziprokopiou 2004:1195; Hatziprokopiou 2003:1041). Pre-existing social networks in Greece or Thessaloniki are a facilitating factor. Friends and relatives already residing there can encourage migration, reduce cost and the risks of leaving and settling in the new environment. Social networks ease the search for employment and residence (Kelly 2005:41; Levitt 2001:8; Phizacklea 2000:127f.; 2003:86; Tastsoglou; Hadjicostanti 2003:195). One third of the women I interviewed had benefited from this.

Thessaloniki`s relative geographic proximity to Albania makes it a favourite destination for Albanian migration. This is a key factor for the development of transnationalism of Albanian migrants residing there (Barjaba, King 2005:20; Fakiolas 2000:64; Labrianidis, Hatziprokopiou 2005:95, 113f.; Tastsoglou, Hadjicostanti 2003:195).

For most of the women, Greece was the only realistic choice, since they want to return to Albania. Nonetheless, one third of them consider Greece only as a temporary destination, their favourite countries would be the USA, Great Britain, Germany and France (in that order). Greece and Italy are the least favoured countries for immigration, due to personal experiences and negative reports by returnees. Countries such as Germany and the USA on the other hand, about which they have no concrete information, fuel their imagination (Prohazka 2002:244). The more distant a country, the more progressive it seems to many Albanians. Thus, the USA is the most favourite country of immigration (Mai 2002:52f.; Prohazka 2003:248).

These women seek a better life not only for themselves, but also for their families, especially for their children. In some instances, their children could only join them later. In cases of illegal immigration, it is difficult for the rest of the family to follow. This family-based motivation is supported by several studies among Albanian domestic servants (Kelly 2005:39, 51; Phizacklea 2000:140). Most women make the migratory decision not from an individual, but from a family perspective:

> "The strong family basis to much migration behaviour in Albania reinforces the importance of kinship, social networks and the ´new economics of migration` approach which stresses ´rational choices` from family/household rather than an individual perspective" (Barjaba, King 2005:20).

This observation seems to contradict neo-classical models, according to which migratory decisions are made by individual rational choice. In the 1980s, household motivation was identified as a primary reason for migration, rather than personal desires. The resulting ´household-strategy-model` is based on three conditions:

> "that households represent shared income, resources and goals; that migration is a reactive strategy to a lack of fit between households consumption and locally available resource and that household-wide decisions are made about migration" (Phizacklea 2000:123).

According to Phizacklea (2000:123), the gender aspect is not sufficiently taken into consideration. Often the elder generation make the migratory decision for the younger members of the family. Increasingly, young women are sent away by the family because the labour of young men is needed at home. Additionally, women are considered as more reliable in their financial support. This development corresponds to the worldwide increased demand for female labour and contributes to the growing feminisation of migration (Phizacklea 2000:121f.; 2003:83).

In summary, there are many factors leading to the migration of Albanian women. The poor economic condition forced many Albanian women to leave their country for Greece in the hope of gaining employment and living a better life. Although Greece is not the prime country of choice, Thessaloniki is often the first destination because many migrants already have transnational relations with relatives and friends there. These networks have a major influence on migratory decisions and are very helpful after arriving in the city. The short geographic distance is also an important factor. Since the majority of the women wants to return to Albania as soon as living conditions become more acceptable, migration to Greece is a temporary strategy to secure economic subsistence for themselves and for the whole family (Labrianidis, Hatziprokopiou 2005:97, 100).

## Return migration: the final goal

The majority of the Albanian women in my study wish to return to their home country as soon as conditions allow and their goals are realised. Return migration, or at least the plan to return, is an integral part of the migratory process. This has been overlooked in the literature for a long time, since migration was seen as a uni-linear movement from the country of origin to the country of residence. In 1995, Albanian migrants of the first wave returned to Albania. After the collapse of the pyramid system, many emigrated again. Official data on Albanian return migration are not available, since these new movements go backward and forward and often have an informal character. For many Albanians, migration and return migration are not permanent conditions, but reversible options (ibid.:93ff.).

Before their immigration, most migrants make plans for their return, but migratory experiences often modify these plans. The possibility of return is time-dependent, but the potential influence of time seems to be ambivalent. The incidence of return migration is reduced with the length of the stay in the country of residence. The reasons are either a gradual integration into the residence society, or migratory goals that could not yet be reached in the imagined time period.

For the women in my study, economic factors were a major prerequisite for returning. Under the present circumstances, they do not feel welcome in Albania. A return can only be realised when the situation there has improved, especially in the labour market. Two women stated in interviews:

> "I think of going back to Albania, I want to, but when I don't know. [...] It is not, that you cannot live there it is about work. If I could find a work, I would be thankful, then I could give up this one. [...] I cannot go there, I am not sure. Certainly, I like it, it is my homeland, there are my parents, my friends, my language which I speak. But now I cannot return, it is difficult to risk that" (Miranda, 35 years).

> "My whole life is there [in Albania]. There I got my children. I like it. If the situation is getting better, we can return, with all that money. I like it, the life, it is my homeland" (Meqi, 45 years).

These statements demonstrate that at present these women cannot imagine living in Albania, although they identify themselves with Albania as their home in which family and friends live, and whose language they speak. The Albanian language is essential for returning. While the generation of the parents has better abilities in Albanian than in Greek, the younger generation writes and speaks Greek better than Albanian. The mastery of the Albanian tongue is seen as an important prerequisite for living in Albania.

To prevent a complete loss of the mother tongue in the second generation, immigrant parents let their children attend evening and weekend courses organised by Albanian associations, but the children are supposed to complete their education in Greece to have better chances in their future.

In summary, return migration depends on a normalising political and economic situation in Albania, as well as on the realisation of goals set for the time in Thessaloniki. Primarily, the women want to earn enough money before their return, to have some financial security in Albania. They want their children to have a school diploma or to complete vocational training in Greece. The coming years will show if Albanian immigrants will actually return or if their wish to return will develop into a myth of return characteristic for the formation of diasporas (Safran 1999:285).

## Working conditions in Thessaloniki

As in the rest of the world the demand for domestic labour in Greece has constantly risen in the last years, providing a source income for migrant women. This increasing demand is caused by changes in family and economic patterns. The time period women need to complete their education has become longer, and their participation in the labour market has risen from 31.2% in 1971 to 47.5% in 1996. Greek women, who traditionally were responsible for the household, the children and the care of the elderly, increasingly pursue professional careers. This double burden is eased by domestic servants. The lack of municipal childcare centres, as well as the traditionally limited willingness of men to work in the household, promote this development. Middle-class households consider domestic servants, especially Filipinas, to be a status symbol. Since the participation of Greek women in the labour market will probably rise in the future, the need for domestic service will remain and increase (Fakiolas 2000:60f.; Lazaridis, Psimenos 2000:181f.; Anthias 2000:26ff.; Lazaridis 2000:56ff.; Anthias, Lazaridis 2000:50; Karakatsanis, Swarts 2003:243ff.; Phizacklea 2000:131ff.; 2003:89). This demand explains the high employment rate of Albanian migrant women in the domestic sector.[26] Upward social mobility is a possibility in the female migratory experience, but disillusionment is more likely. Seven of the thirteen women in my study had been without work after their arrival in Greece for a period of up to five years. Four of them are still unemployed. They consider a poor knowledge of the Greek language, lack of time because of household work and care for their children, as well as difficulties in looking for work to be the reason for their unemployment. One woman described her experiences with the Greek labour market:

> "I was without job for four years. It was very difficult, these four years. Four years I was without job, because my language is not good. [...] I was a teacher in Albania, but here it was unbelievable to find a job like a teacher. I should work in a cloth industry, but I didn't know the job. I worked there for one day, or two days, and the third day I was out, they pushed out me, something like this. And for four years I didn't find a job. And then I should learn the Greek, it was necessary for me, and I gave examinations in university for Greek language. Then I could read the jobs in the newspapers, and so I could find a job." (Vlora, 33 years)

For most Albanian women, working as a domestic servant is the only possibility of employment in Greece. Although a job as a domestic servant can be found through job ads in newspapers, having "the right connections" is the usual way to find a job. The tasks of domestic servants include typical household chores and sometimes additional care for children and elderly persons. The physically demanding labour of housecleaning can lead to health problems, which limit their ability to find work. This becomes even more serious by the fact that many women have no health insurance, days in which they cannot work must be compensated for later on, and medical costs have to be paid in full. Because of poor working conditions and low wages, the women in my study were not satisfied with their work. The majority of domestic servants work six days a week in up to thirteen households. They work an average of eight hours per day, in exceptions up to twelve hours, earning between fifteen and forty Euro per day. They have neither work contracts

[26] About half of the women in my study worked as domestic servants, another three were without employment and further three pursued occupations with higher qualifications. One is a journalist working for an Albanian newspaper who offers Albanian courses in her spare time. Another one is involved in a social work project against the trafficking of children, works as a teacher for Greek in a Greek school, and gives courses in Albanian. The third woman also teaches Albanian besides running a textile shop with her husband. These three women show possibilities for female migrants beyond the informal sector.

nor old age pensions. Due to their long workday and their six day week, they have little spare time.

Due to the absence of employee protection, financial security or a health plan, domestic servants are powerless and vulnerable. This condition can easily lead to exploitation. Migrants without residence permit are even more dependent on their employers. According to Lazaridis, the establishment of social networks allows domestic workers to escape this vulnerability at least to a certain degree and ensure some sort of upward social mobility. Current studies show an Albanian community presently being established in Thessaloniki. Social networks increase migrants´ visibility in the public and reach more migrants. During the last years, a positive tendency in the development of working and living conditions of Albanian migrants has been documented (Anthias 2000:26f.; Hatziprokopiou 2004:1052f.; Lazaridis 2000:63ff., 69f., 73; Lazaridis, Psimenos, 2000:179; Karakatsanis, Swarts, 2003:247f., 260f.; Phizacklea 2000:145).

Through their participation in the labour market, migration of women can change gender relations within the family. The role of women as keepers of tradition and culture, especially in patriarchal society, can be reduced or strengthened in the migratory context, where they assume new economic and social roles (Kelly 2005:34). Changed gender relations can result in a gain or a loss of power. The position of women is weakened if they are unable to work, unable to speak the language of the country of residence, or isolated from extended family networks. On the other hand, new social and economic responsibilities by entering the labour market, can be the basis for a stronger position of women in the family. Paid work implies learning the local language and acquiring new skills and knowledge, an independent personal income, and can bring more independence and self-confidence. "Immigrant women can use their role as money-earners to achieve a different position within their families and hence modify gender roles“ (Campani 2000:148).

In her study of Dominican migrants in Boston, Levitt noted the influence of transnational social networks on gender relations, also among family members, relatives and friends who remained at home. Behaviour, norms and values of women changed as a reaction to their active participation in the labour market, confrontation with the school system, and other public services. These new norms and identities were transferred to women in the Dominican Republic through transnational relations, constructing a new local version of womanhood (Levitt 2001:61, 97ff.).

A special feature of Albanian migration is the fact that Albanian women were already working during the Hoxha regime (Kelly 2005:35). The political and economic transformation during the post-communist period had an important influence on gender relations within Albanian family patterns. As in other post-communist countries, during transformation a traditional division of labour among family members was reactivated. As in the pre-communist era, women were expected to stay at home while men again became the sole provider of income. The tensions caused by this process were expressed in the high divorce rate (Kaser 2000:49, 53). Traditional family roles were once again challenged by migration. Active participation in the labour market, an independent income, the acquisition of new skills and knowledge enabled Albanian migrant women to solidify their position within the family which had been weakened in the post-communist years.

In summary, employment in the resident country was of significant importance for the women in my study. Primarily, they had migrated to Greece to secure their own economic survival and that of their whole family. Work is a necessary means of achieving the financial basis for a better future in Albania.

## Social networks and Albanian associations in Thessaloniki

Social networks consisting of family, household and community relations are essential for the migratory decision:

> "Once migration begins these networks come to function as causes of migration themselves because they lower the costs and risks of migration and increase the expected returns on migration" (Phizacklea 2000:128).

In the migratory environment, personal social networks and institutionalized associations are crucial for settling, for employment, and for maintaining ties to the homeland.

Research in Athens, on Corfu and in Thessaloniki shows significant differences relating to networks and organizations. According to Lazaridis, there are hardly any Albanian associations in Athens and on Corfu, but Hatziprokopiou described their existence in Thessaloniki (Hatziprokopiou 2003:1051f.). So far, the low public visibility of Albanian associations makes it difficult for many Albanian migrants to take advantage of them. Informal social networks such as extended family, friends and neighbours are also essential for settling, finding work and accommodation, as well as for maintaining ties to the country of origin (Lazaridis, Psimenos 2000:179; Phizacklea 2003:86).

Albanian associations founded in Thessaloniki during the 1990s serve a dual purpose. On the one hand, they facilitate daily life in the country of residence (job search and social contacts), on the other hand they maintain contact to Albania, by reproducing elements of the home culture such as Albanian newspapers, Albanian language courses and Albanian festive events. These ties with the home country strengthen the wish to return. For Phizacklea, celebrating homeland holidays, cooking homeland food, and performing homeland dances are important examples of transnational actions (2003:80f.).

*Albanians in Thessaloniki*, the oldest Albanian association in Thessaloniki, was founded in 1998. It is located in Vardaris, in the west of Thessaloniki near the harbour in the house of a workers` association. Textile stores of Chinese immigrants are predominant in this part of the city. The association is not officially registered, but is integrated in an evening school offering courses for migrants in Greek, English and computer science. In 2003, the largest group attending this school was Albanian (40%), in the meantime, Asian migrants constitute the majority. The association is a meeting place for

Location of *Albanians in Thessaloniki* (Photo: Elke Haas)

Albanian migrants, offering help with legal affairs and occupational matters. *Albanians in Thessaloniki* cooperates with an anti-racist group located in the centre of the city which was founded in 1996. Since 1998, an anti-racist festival, in which migrants from different countries such as Georgia, the Sudan and the Philippines participate, is organized each year by both groups. They also offer Albanian language courses on Sundays, for the second generation of Albanian migrants: "Since 2001 until now, we are holding Albanian language courses for our children [...]. We teach the children for free, we do it for the children, we teach them our language, because they do not know it any more. And this is the problem for migrants, they do not learn their mother language" (Miranda, 35 years).

Albanian language course (Photo: Elke Haas)

In cooperation with a Greek publishing house, the association publishes the Albanian newspaper *Vezhguesi* (Albanian: perspective, look). In 2002 an Albanian radio programme was created with the help of the publishing house. The association is part of a federation of Albanian associations in Greece and organizes competitions in the literary and graphic arts, a culinary festival, as well as intercultural sporting events.

The *Mother Tereza* association was formed in May/June 2004 after the first Albanian association had split up. It also supports Albanian migrants in legal, financial and occupational matters, offers Albanian language courses as well as musical development, and it provides a playroom for children. This association is in contact with the Greek non-governmental organisation ARSIS[27] and organizes discussions, picnics, football games, parties and Albanian national celebrations.

[27] Association for the Support of the Youth

In summary, Albanian associations in Thessaloniki provide many services for migrants which are the basis for the constitution of community life. They offer support in legal and financial matters, as well as in finding work, and are maintaining the culture and language of the home country. By remaining in contact with their home culture, migrants keep their Albanian identification which strengthens their wish to return. Thus, the associations promote the transnational character of Albanian migration.

## Transnational practices of Albanian migrant women

Transnationalism is encouraged by geographic proximity, the wish to return, family financial responsibilities and emotional ties, as well as by social networks in the place of residence. It is practiced in the form of regular cross-border travel and communication, as well as financial and material support. The majority of the women in my study visited Albania on a regular basis. Almost half of them travelled to Albania once a year, either for the winter or summer holidays. One quarter travels twice or more often per year. The duration of stay is between two and twenty-five days.

Transnational mobility is influenced by two factors: personal motivation and business. One woman is working as a social worker for Albanian street children in Thessaloniki, whose parents she is trying to find in Albania. Another woman is a journalist working for an Albanian newspaper published in Greece. The tendency to travel to Albania is greater for those who have a legal permit to stay. An unclear status prevented one woman from crossing the border in the first three years of her stay in Greece.

Geographic proximity and the availability of different forms of transportation ease transnational mobility (Labrianidis, Hatziprokopiou 2005:114). Transport routes are readily available for legal immigrants since Albania is only a few hours from Thessaloniki by bus, car or taxi. The majority of the women and their families normally use the bus to travel either to Korçe in Southern Albania or the centrally located capital, Tirana. The bus trip to Korçe takes approximately five hours and costs twenty Euro, to Tirana ten hours for thirty Euro. The rest of the women use motorcars, rarely taxis. As I was informed, another alternative is crossing the border on foot. This method is mainly used by men who cross the border illegally.

The majority of the women provide material or financial support for their families in Albania. As one of them stressed, for migrants this support is "the natural thing to do". In general, remittances are an important aspect of transnational support for migrants, especially for migrant women. The family based migratory decision makes the women responsible for the family that was left behind (Anthias 2000:31).

As Labrianidis et al. and Hatziprokopiou note, almost 50% of Albanian migrants in Thessaloniki support their families in Albania financially (Labrianidis, Lyberaki, Tinios, Hatziprokopiou 2004:1197; Hatziprokopiou 2003:1041). This was also the case for all women in my study. To secure this financial support, those crossing the border can take cash with them. Relatives or friends can also perform this service. Only recently, some banks in Greece offer transfer of remittances to Albania.

In general, economic support by Albanian migrants is crucial for the survival of Albanian society. Since 1995, the total remittance of Albanian immigrants was estimated between 300 million and one billion Dollars per year. Second to foreign aid, this is the largest source of foreign income for Albania, amounting to one third of the GDP (gross domestic product), and equal to more than half of the income from exports. Therefore, remittances of Albanian migrants have been a key factor in the social and economic development of the country. Despite the low income of Albanian migrants in their country of residence in relation to indigenous workers, it is sufficient to support up to five people in Albania. The complete collapse of the social support mechanisms during the post-communist transition increased the economic importance of Albanian migration even more (Barjaba, King 2005:21f.; Mai, Schwandner-Sievers 2003:940ff.; Phizacklea 2003:85f.; Piperno 2005:119).

Since female Albanian migrants have little money at their disposal, there is a tendency to provide support for their family in the form of material goods. There are different possibilities to transport goods to Albania, either bringing them personally when they visit, or sending them by bus. In this case, they give them to the bus driver who demands ten Euro for this service. They can also give them to relatives and friends travelling to Albania. The postal service is most costly and therefore seldom used. Transnational communication is another form of practicing transnationalism. On the average, all of the interviewed women communicated with family members in Albania once a week per telephone. E-mail was not used.

In summary, the women in my study remained in contact with their home country through regular communication with family members by telephone (on the average once a week) and by personal visits (on the average once or twice per year). Financial and material support for their family in Albania is maintained, as this was the main motivation for their migratory decision. Remittances invested in Albania, as well as personal contacts, are supposed to secure return migration and a better life in Albania in the future.

## Conclusion: transnationalism as strategy

Albanian women migrate to Thessaloniki to improve their economic situation and that of their families. The migratory decision is usually made by the whole family. There is a worldwide tendency of households to send young women abroad, since the labour force of young men is needed at home and women seem to be the more reliable senders of remittances. Thus, the migration of women has been increasing.

This is also the case for Albanian migration. Albanian women want better living conditions, not just for the present time in Greece, but for a future life in Albania, to where they want to return as soon as they have saved enough money. The high number of domestic servants in my study corresponds with the worldwide increased demand in the domestic service sector. The feminisation of migration has led to women playing an increasingly important role in the survival of Albanian society. Their reliable remittances to their families in Albania provide financial security.

Social networks in Greece facilitate immigration, settlement in the country of residence and return migration. Albanian association promote identification with the home country by celebrating Albanian holidays, dancing Albanian dances, cooking Albanian food and teaching the Albanian language. These particular forms of transnationalism strengthen the wish of Albanian migrants to return by keeping Albania in their minds. Concrete transnational practices (communication, border-crossings and support of the family in Albania) are the key factor for maintaining ties to Albania. Thus, geographic proximity between the country of origin and of residence, the availability of transportation, economic and emotional ties to family members and friends left behind in Albania, Albanian associations in the country of residence, as well as concrete transnational actions determine the transnational character of Albanian female migration. As Labrianidis and Hatziprokopiou recently stated, transnational networks even persist after returning:

> "These informal social networks link people who live in different places and [...] such links continue to exist after migrants return: either with relatives and friends still abroad, or with Greek and Italian friends and colleagues. [...] This trend, easily observed in the Albanian case, might be more widespread in coming years, as transnational structures become more consolidated" (Labrianidis, Hatziprokopiou 2005:114f.).

# The Jewish Community of Thessaloniki

Sarah Brammann

This paper deals with the Jewish community of Thessaloniki and the changes it has been going through within the last fifteen years. In her fieldwork in the late 1980s, Beate Lewkowicz studied identity processes and representations among the young members of the Jewish community. Fifteen years later, I was intrigued by the obvious changes that had occurred in the community's public image. But besides academic interest, private matters also have influenced my choice of the topic. Growing up with my mother´s Jewish partner, who took over the father role, my interest in Jewish religion and culture has been sparked early. These two factors have predisposed my interest in the subject matter and have led me to formulate my central research questions.

The main focus of my field work was based on prior research by Beate Lewkowicz (1990a and b). I start by introducing her results, proceeding with an overview of the historical background of the Sephardic community of Thessaloniki, which still plays a significant role in the process of identity construction and the representation of a Jewish cityscape. Based on a description of the community's representation today, I will discuss aspects influencing current changes, focusing on social relations as a central factor of Jewish identity. Similar to Lewkowicz´s study, my fieldwork was also based on interviews and observations among younger members of the Jewish community, mostly aged between eighteen and thirty.

Lewkowicz (1990a and b) describes the endurance of the Jewish community as depending on the personal commitment and awareness of Jewish identity among the younger members of the community, while demographic data show an overrepresentation of the elder generation (Lewkowicz 1990b:86f.).

According to Lewkowicz, not just religious affiliations but the social network one is born into, and a common feeling of belonging to a diaspora in Greece, motivate the member's activities and enable the community's enduring survival (ibid.:93). Jewish identity, according to Lewkowicz, is confronted by strong Greek nationalism and a strong pressure of assimilation (ibid.:82). Accommodating both Greek and Jewish identities nonetheless is enabled by a praxis Lewkowicz has labelled *'private Judaism'*. In her article, she suggests that the self-images of young community members and the public profile of the community correspond to each other and need to be understood as mutually complementing elements (Lewkowicz 1994:236). The potential conflict of being Jewish in a Greek-orthodox society is abrogated by living the Jewish part of one's identity only in the private sphere. Consequently, the Jewish identity will be questioned in the long run, as Lewkowicz assumes (Lewkowicz 1990b:95).

At the time of her field work, the Jewish community hardly presented itself in public at all. Neither the three-story community centre was recognizable to outsiders, nor was there any memorial for the victims of the Holocaust or any reference to the former Jewish cemetery, which was destroyed in the Holocaust and is now the campus of Aristotele University.

## Historical Overview

Jewish presence in Thessaloniki is documented throughout the entire history of the city (Spengler-Axiopoulos 1998:2), until the Sephardic[28] community was almost annihilated during the Holocaust (Mazower 2004: 438) Today only the generation of the survivors speak *Ladino* (Judeo-Spanish).

Spanish Jews who resisted compulsory Christianisation in the end of the 15th century, were expelled from Spain and found refuge in the Ottoman Empire. After 1492, more than 20 000 Jews arrived in the city as refugees from the Iberian Peninsula. Sephardic Jews also settled in other parts of the Ottoman Empire during this time (Spengler-Axiopoulos 1992:2f.; Molho 1991:110). Sephardic Judaism became predominant in the city's Jewish communities (Spengler-Axiopoulos 1992:4). Sephardic self-assurance

[28] Most studies of the Jewish community in Thessaloniki have only dealt with the Sephardic history of Thessaloniki, while data dealing with the Jews before 1492 are rare and rather conflicting. From a historical perspective, there is a broad spectrum of literature about the Sephardic community up to the year 1980, dealing explicitly with the construction of identity and the Jewish cityscape of Thessaloniki (cf. also Lewkowicz 1990b; 1994; 2006).

expressed itself in several proverbs, such as: "*Basta mi nombre es Abravanel*", meaning as much as: "my (Sephardic) good name is sufficient, I don´t need to give any more guarantees"(ibid.: 4).

During the Ottoman Empire, Sephardic Jews were respected specialists in medicine, arms technology or printing, but they also were merchants or craftsmen. Jewish merchants and tailors were privileged suppliers of uniforms to the Janissary Corps, the elite military force of the Sultan (Spengler-Axiopoulos 1998: 3).

In the middle of the 19th century, Thessaloniki was connected to Europe via railway from Vienna to Istanbul. At the same time, the port of Thessaloniki was modernized and tramways were running in the city. Jewish companies contributed significantly to the industrialization of Thessaloniki. In 1860, the *Alliance Israélite Universelle* was founded to bring the idea of emancipation and enlightenment closer to the Jews of the Orient. In 1873, the first school of the AIU in Thessaloniki was established. Lessons were taught in French, which also contributed to the disappearance of Ladino as a literary language. The AIU published every case of anti-Semitism in the Middle East and in North Africa, enabled by a substantial communication network, even using telegraphy. At the same time, the *Féderation,* a socialist labour movement, emerged in Thessaloniki as the only labour movement emerging in Sephardic history. The dominating role of Jewish labourers is to be explained by the high share of Jews in the population of Thessaloniki, also in the working class. The *Féderation* published two newspapers, *Solidaridad Ovradera* and *Journal de Labrador* (Spengler-Axiopoulos 1992).

Thessaloniki was incorporated into the Greek State in 1912. In contrast to the Christian population, the Jewish community lost some of their privileges, e.g. the exemption from military service and municipal self-administration. In consequence, the Zionist Movement gained foothold in the Jewish population. In 1919, the first Zionist congress took place in Thessaloniki (Molho 1991:114; Spengler-Axiopoulos 1998:6). The administration of King George of Greece showed positive interest in Jewish efforts to proclaim a Jewish nation state. However, as the historian Rena Molho (1988, 2001) points out, anti-semitism was present in Greece even before the German invasion.

In 1917 a great fire destroyed wide parts of the inner city, including many Jewish neighbourhoods. The former residents were compelled to move to suburbs and lived under miserable conditions:

> "The Jewish community was worst affected for the fire had consumed the historic quarters: most of its thirty-seven synagogues were gone, its libraries, schools, club buildings and offices. " (Mazower 2004:320)

In 1923, over 1.5 million Greek refugees were expelled from Asia Minor, more than 100 000 of them settled in Thessaloniki (Molho 1991:119; Mazower 2004:363-365). In 1924 the Sabbath was abolished and the Christian sunday was introduced in Thessaloniki. In 1926, extreme nationalist organisations called for a boycott of all Jewish businesses. After a neighbourhood inhabited by Jewish refugees from the great fire of 1917 was attacked and sacked, more than 10 000 Jews emigrated to Palestine in reaction to the pogrome. In 1936, many Jewish associations were banned (Spengler-Axiopoulos 1992:11-13).

After Thessaloniki was occupied by the German Wehrmacht on the 9th of April 1941, agitation and persecutions against Jews began almost immediately (Mazower 2004: 421-423). Jewish press organs were confiscated and in July 1942. Ninethousend Jews were conscripted to forced labour. From March to August 1943, Jews of Thessaloniki were deported to Auschwitz (Mazower 2004:431-433).

Throughout its history, Sephardic influence had formed the city's appearance, but after the Holocaust the Jewish community was reduced to a marginal size:

> "Almost no Jews (now) remained in Thessaloniki. Fifteen or so were exempted because they were married to non-Jews – some well-connected Greek men with Jewish wives had protested angrily to the Germans and managed to save their families – and up to one hundred were hiding with friends. Two women were helped by men they later married; another older woman was hidden by a Christian relative. An unknown number of children were adopted...." (Mazower 2004:438)

Of 46 091 Jews deported to the extermination camps, only 1950 returned alive (Foundation for the Advancement of Sephardic Studies and Culture 2007:3). Of about 48 000 Jews of Thessaloniki previous to the beginning of the war, only 2000 returned after the war was over (Spengler-Axiopoulos 1992:18).

## The present: community structure and activities

Today, the Jewish community has about 1000 members. Four times a week, service is administered at a synagogue close to the *Stoa Modiano* market hall (Schwalgin 1995). The community runs a retirement home for the elderly with about forty inhabitants at the time of my field work, a primary school, and a kindergarten. The *Monasteriotes* synagogue was not destroyed in World War II, since the Red Cross used it as a warehouse during that time. This synagogue is only used for the celebration of the main holydays. An second synagogue, *Yad Ledzicaron*, which is used for Sabbath prayer was opened in 1984 in dedication to the victums of the Holocaust (Jewish Community of Thessaloniki 1996).

Entrance of the Yad Ledzicaron Synagogue
(Photo: Sarah Brammann)

Various activities are offered to the community members, including a cultural club, a sports club and an association promoting closer bonds between Israel and Greece (Spengler-Axiopoulos 1992:18-21; Foundation for the Advancement of Sephardic Studies and Culture 2007:1). As a Legal Entity under Public Law, the Jewish Community is subject to control by the Ministries of Education and Religion. Every four years, the twenty-member Community Assembly is elected, which in turn elects the five-member Community Council. This council is in charge of establishing different committees of the different sections, such as primary school and synagogues (Foundation for the Advancement of Sephardic Studies and Culture 2007: 1).

The new Jewish Museum is located in an impressing complex of buildings in the centre of the city. It is one of the few structures in the commercial district that were not destroyed by the great fire of 1917 (Jewish Museum of Thessaloniki 2005). Once the Bank of Athens, later the Jewish newspaper *L'independent* had its domicile here. Situated in this district, it is only one of the numerous examples of the community's former presence in Thessaloniki. The Museum was founded in 1997 in order to document the comprehensive Jewish heritage of the city. The building was renovated by the Cultural Capital of Europe Organization "Thessaloniki 1997". Two floors of the building are used for exhibitions.

Museum of the Jewish Presence in Thessaloniki (Photo: Sarah Brammann)

The new Jewish Museum exemplifies a significant change in the self-representation of the Jewish community. At the time of Lewkowicz´s research, Jewish presence in Thessaloniki was virtually invisible. While being Jewish was of utmost importance for her informants´ social relations and feelings of identity, this was hardly presented at all in non-Jewish contexts. Being Jewish was considered a private affair, and even religious rituals that are supposed to be performed in public were confined within the walls of the synagogue. According to Lewkowicz, the reasons for this extreme caution lie not only in the devastating experience of the Holocaust, but also in the precarious position of a diaspora community in relation to the demands of the Greek nation-state.

In 2004, this situation has changed. Although potential conflicts still exist in being Jewish in Greek society, young community members no longer feel forced to live the Jewish part of their identity exclusively in the private sphere. Different from the late 1980es, today´s young generation seems to face fewer restrictions in presenting their Jewish identity and cultural practice in public. Nonetheless, for this generation as for the one described by Lewkowicz, Jewish social relations and institutionalised networking remain essential factors in strengthening personal and community identity.

Consequently, I suggest that the Jewish community's identity has not diminished, as predicted by Lewkowicz (1990b). Instead, it has been reinforced - influenced by, as well as influencing, the community's self-presentation in public.

## Social aspects of Jewish identity

The concept of "Judaism" not only refers to a religious affiliation, but also to a coherent social community. As Rothschild (2002) suggests, the denomination "Jewish" refers to all persons belonging to Jewish communities, but it also applies to persons who are born Jewish, but who have disassociated themselves from community structures or live far away from active communities, but could be members if they wanted to (Rothschild 2002:10).

In the course of my fieldwork, my informants consistently pointed out that this social/relational feature of Judaism was particularly important to them. For most of them, it was not predominatly religious belief, but the social aspects of community life that constituted their Jewish identity. All of my interview partners drew attention to this point, except for one who did not actively take part in community life.

The community offers its members various possibilities of participation. There are readings and meetings, where different topics related to Jewry can be discussed. Besides the retirement home and the primary school, there is a Ladino Centre offering courses and Ladino studies (Straub 2000:496). Children and young community members can attend classes for religious education held by the Rabbi. The Jewish community of Thessaloniki is linked to other communities in Greece and Europe, and to a world wide network of Jewish Communities. In "youth summer camps" and during excursions, members of different communities in and beyond Greece can meet each other. Every Friday, young community members meet for a ceremony celebrating the beginning of the Sabbath where they can play games together, talk and have fun. This gathering strengthens the social bonds among the younger generation.

Even community members who do not describe themselves as religious take part in community activities. As the chairman of the Youth Club told me in an interview, most young community members were not ardently religious, but the social bonds became more and more important to them. An encompassing discourse of preserving the community and ensuring its survival constitutes a significant part of the members´ identity, which is in turn closely linked to the community´s representation in public.

According to my interview partners, community members feel obliged to support each other both in business and in private matters. Community members are preferred as partners in commercial operations, due to the fact that the families have known each other for generations and their children have grown up together. On the basis of common religious education, enduring friendships exist from childhood on. Consistently my interview partners mentioned the importance of these social bonds. For most of them, being Jewish is a significant part of their daily lives, influencing many spheres of action. One of my informants explained it as an attitude of life: "It's the feeling of being Jewish, not the religion, but the feeling" (Moshe, 27 years old). Starting from school days, as my informants told me, they had always been "special" in a way. Most of my informants explained that it is very important to strengthen the social bonds within the community, in order to preserve Jewish life and culture in Thessaloniki. As one of my interview partners pointed out explicitly: "I want to preserve our identity, inheritance is very strong, and I am not going to destroy the Jewish community of Thessaloniki. I am going to do everything to preserve it." (Elias, 28 years old).

It is important to note however, that during my field work in Thessaloniki, I predominantly met young community members who actively participated in community life. It was not possible for me to contact young Jews who had distanced themselves from community acitivities. This may influence the great emphasis on social relations as factors of Jewish identity in the statements of my informants.

In summary, social relations still constitute a central aspect of community identity, both as a concept and as a practice. Community life offers social connectivity and solidarity, which are not only based on religious belief and practice, but on friendship and corporate relations over generations. For most members also of the young generation, preserving the community is part of a communal duty constituting the core of their membership. In return, the community offers protection and familiarity from childhood on.

## The problem of mixed marriages

In numerically small communities like Thessaloniki, it is not easy for young people to find a Jewish partner. In addition, the younger generation is not getting married at such an early age as their parents and grandparents[29]. While most of the older generation married when they were about twenty years old, the second generation after the war marries on the average in their late twenties or beginning of their thirties. Although most married couples have children, the birth rate has been decreasing. My interview partners told me that for eight community members who have died, only one child is born into the community. This also has consequences for the education of the children. Since the birth rate is sinking constantly, there are less children of the same age to attend school in one class. Therefore, only few parents send their children to the Jewish primary school, while other parents argue that the classes are too small to provide an adequate social environment in this school.

All but one of my informants explicitly stated that while relationships with non-Jewish partners might be possible for them, they would not consider a mixed marriage. Diverse reasons were named for this, most importantly the fear of a breach in the family. In the generation of my informants´ parents and grandparents, marriages "between the religions" are generally not approved of. If mixed marriages do occur, they are observed critically. A marriage with a woman who has converted to Judaism is regarded as only a second choice, because of fear that the woman might convert back to her original faith after all. The majority of my interview partners argued that it was bad for children to grow up "between the religions". The child would not develop a proper orientation towards religious beliefs and practices. This was also implied in cases of parents deciding to educate the child in the Jewish religion only, because the Christian in-laws could still influence the religious affiliation of the child in other ways. This potential conflict was symbolized by an anecdote, told to me by several of my informants: two grandmothers

[29] The figures quoted are based on estimations by my interview partners. Regrettably, I did not have access to any statistics on this topic.

are kneeling at the baby's cradle, one grandmother draws symbolically a cross on the baby's chest, while the other grandmother is putting a necklace with a *Magen David*, (Star of David) over the baby's head.

It was of prime importance to all of my male interview partners to pass on the family name. A member of the Youth Club Committee told me that he was the last of his family carrying the name, therefore he had to marry to pass on the name. For this reason, the woman would have to bear him a son. Another informant, who was already married, also explained that for him the crucial reason for choosing his wife had been the fact that she was Jewish. Again, it is important to note a significant bias in my field work: all but one of my interview partners were men[30] .

Dealing with the subject of mixed marriages, my informants were always talking of marriages between Jews and Orthodox Christians. Mixed marriages between other confessions were not considered at all. Marriages between Jews and Moslems were excluded in the discussion and viewed as completely impossible.

During my fieldwork, I did not have access to any statistics about the actual number of mixed marriages, but my informants´ statements point to some possible discrepancies between the stated desire for Jewish partners, and demographic realities. About one-third of the members of Thessaloniki´s Jewish community are between 18 and 35 years old. The small size of the community makes it hard to find a Jewish partner in Thessaloniki. Various possibilities are offered to meet new people and to find a husband or wife from outside of the community. Many young people visit Summer Universities, join the summer camps or participate in youth club activities all over Greece. Nevertheless, my informants reported that every second marriage is a mixed marriage, although this was not affirmed by the official community administration.

According to Lewkowicz, "the issue of mixed marriage is very delicate because it is regarded by many as a symbol of undesirable assimilation." (Lewkowicz 1994:231). She argues that although most informants did not explicitly disapprove of the relationship of

[30] According to Jewish law, a person is Jewish if he or she is born by a Jewish mother, or if he or she converted to Judaism (Rothschild 2002:10)

the couple, their disapproval was directed towards the situation of the children in a mixed marriage. In 2004, this does not seem to have changed. In summary, the majority of my informants gave similar statements on this topic, with the difference that my informants were critical or disapproving of mixed marriages not only regarding the education of the children. All of my interview partners desired a marriage with a Jewish partner, emphasising the need for preservation of the Jewish community. I see this emphasis as a further aspect of the social relevance of Judaism. The explicit refusal of mixed marriages by young community members strengthens the community by admitting to their religion and culture in public. By stating the intention of in-group marriage as a personal goal, one's individual biography is connected to a communal identity.

## Public representation of the Jewish community today

The public representation of the Jewish community of Thessaloniki has distinctly changed within the last fifteen years. Now it is the community's explicit aim, as I was told, not only to preserve the community by keeping the memory of Sephardic culture in Thessaloniki, but to open this memory to a wider public. These intentions are epitomized by the Museum of Jewish Presence in Thessaloniki.

While Jewish presence was still quite invisible to the Greek public at the time of Lewkowicz´ fieldwork, in the last years there have been numerous activities representing the community to a wider audience. In 1990, Lewkowicz quoted the former president arguing against a memorial tablet to the victims of the Holocaust, because he feared that it would be disgraced by anti-semitic graffitis anyway (Lewkowicz 1990b:94). This policy of making oneself "invisible" has changed significanty. The present president of the community, David Saltiel, stated in a press interview that the memory of the Jewish presence in Thessaloniki must be reanimated. In the same interview, Saltiel elaborated how the Jewish community of Thessaloniki and Sephardic culture should regain public awareness:

> „Schritt für Schritt versuchen wir wieder bekannt zu machen, dass in dieser Stadt das jüdische Element eine entscheidende Rolle gespielt hat – in Kultur und Handel. Thessaloniki war tatsächlich Zentrum des Balkans und wird es

wieder sein nach dem Beitritt der südosteuropäischen Länder in die EU. Wir haben vor einigen Jahren ein Museum errichtet, der Gedenktag wurde letztes Jahr eingeführt. All dies sind Faktoren, die uns helfen, die Menschen wieder darüber zu informieren, was war und welche Rolle die jüdische Gemeinde spielte."[31] (Athener Zeitung 2006: Interview with Albert Spiegel and David Saltiel)

As Saltiel declares, the community's efforts focus on raising public awareness about the role of Jewish culture in history of Thessaloniki. The founding of the museum and the introduction of a Memorial Day are two steps in this programme. Preserving the community and representing it in public, is tied up to the memory of the Holocaust. Sixty years after the end of World War II, the Greek parliament has declared the day of deliverance of Auschwitz as a commemoration day for Jewish inhabitants of Thessaloniki.

Further efforts to enhance the community's public visibility include the endeavour to establish a professorship for Sephardic Studies in the University of Thessaloniki (Newspaper of Athens 2006: Interview with Albert Spiegel and David Saltiel). Today Ladino is thought in the Community Centre once a week. In 2004, the Jewish community demanded the integration of the Jewish history of Thessaloniki into the curriculum of public schools (Neuber 2005).

## Conclusion

In the previous article I have described aspects of continuity and change in the Jewish community of Thessaloniki. Taking Lewkowicz´s research as a point of departure, I have noted that social relations within the community, as well as the issue of mixed marriages, are still of prime importance to the younger generation. However, the need for "private Judaism" as described by Lewkowicz in the late 1980es seems to have diminished, as

[31] „Step by step we try to make known once more the supreme role, which the Jewish element has been playing in this city - in culture and in trade. Indeed, Thessaloniki was the centre of the Balkans and it will become the centre again, after the countries of south-eastern Europe join the EU. We have opened a museum a few years ago, and last year a memorial day was introduced. All these factors will help to inform the people once again about the past and about the role of the Jewish community."

the community´s public presence has changed from near-invisibility to explicit new efforts of public representation.

Numerous projects have been organized in relation to the nomination of Thessaloniki as European Cultural Capital in 1997. A second museum is planned at the old railway station, from where thousands of Jews had been deported to concentration camps (Neuber 2005). Young community members participate actively in representing the Jewish Community in public and put efforts in preserving the community.

Further research will be needed to keep track of the public efforts of the Jewish Community of Thessaloniki and its reception in the Greek public. Comparative research could give insights into the question if this process is only happening in Thessaloniki, or eventually will extend to other Jewish communities as well.

# Literature cited

**Abels, Heinz** (1991) ‚Annäherung an eine Vernichtung. Zur Struktur der biographischen Erzählung einer Überlebenden des Völkermords an den Armeniern'. *Bios. Zeitschrift für Biographieforschung und Oral History* 2/91: 159-190.

**Agelopoulos, Georgios** (2000) 'Political practices and multiculturalism: the case of Salonica', In: Jane Cowan (ed.) *Macedonia. The Politics of Identity and Difference*. London: 140-155.

**Agtizidis, Vlasis** (1991) 'The Persecution of Pontic Greeks in the Soviet Union'. *Journal of Refugee Studies* 4/4, 1991: 372-381.

**Anthias, Floya** (2000) 'Metaphors of Home: Gendering new migration to southern Europe', In: Floya Anthias, Gabriella Lazaridis (eds.) *Gender and Migration in Southern Europe: Women on the Move.* Oxford, New York: 15-48.

**Anthias, Floya; Lazaridis, Gabriella** (2000) 'Introduction: women on the move in Southern Europe', In: F. Anthias, G. Lazaridis (eds.) *Gender and Migration in Southern Europe: Women on the Move.* Oxford, New York: 1-14.

**Apospori, Eleni** (2003) 'The dynamics of poverty and multidimensional deprivation in Greece', In: Eleni Apospori, Jane Millar (eds.) *The Dynamics of Social Exclusion in Europe. Comparing Austria, Germany, Greece, Portugal and the UK.* Cheltenham: 87-113.

**Baratta, Mario von** (2000) *Der Fischer Weltalmanach 2001*. Frankfurt a.M.

**Barbaja, Kosta; King, Russell** (2005) 'Introducing and theorising Albanian migration'. In: Russell King, Nicola Mai ; Stephanie Schwandner-Sievers (eds.) *The New Albanian Migration.* Brighton, Portland: 1-28.

**BBC News** 2001: ‚Greek sex industry uncovered'
http://news.bbc.co.uk/1/hi/world/europe/1724057.stm [November 30 2003].

**Beer, Bettina** (ed.) (2003) *Methoden und Techniken der Feldforschung.* Berlin.

**Bernard, Harvey Russell** (2006) *Research methods in anthropology : qualitative and quantitative approaches.* Lanham.

**Bernard, Harvey Russell** (ed.) (2000) *Handbook of methods in cultural anthropology.* Walnut Creek, CA.

**Bryer, Anthony** (1991) 'The Pontic Greeks before the Diaspora'. *Journal of Refugee Studies* 4/4, 1991: 315-334.

**Campani, Giovanna** (2000) 'Immigrant women in southern Europe: social exclusion, domestic work and prostitution in Italy'. In: Russell King, Gabriella Lazaridis, Charalambos Tsardanidis (eds.), *Eldorado or Fortress? Migration in Southern Europe.* New York: 147-169.

**Campbell, John Kennedy** (1964) *Honor, family and patronage. A study of institutions and moral values in a Greek mountain community.* Oxford.

**Cavounidis, Jennifer** (2003) 'Gendered patterns of migration to Greece'. *The Greek Review of Social Research.* 110: 221-238.

**Clogg, Richard** (1979) A *short history of modern Greece.* Cambridge.

**Commission Of The European Communities** 2003: ‚Communication From The Commission To The Council, The European Parliament, The European Economic And Social Committee And The Committee Of The Regions: Joint Report On Social Inclusion. Summarising The Results Of The Examination Of The National Action Plans For Social Inclusion (2003-2005)': http://eur-lex.europa.eu/LexUriServ/site/en/com/2003/com2003_0773en01.pdf [April 14 2006].

**Cowan, Jane K.** 1991: 'Going out for Coffee? Contesting the Grounds of Gendered Pleasures in Everyday Sociability'. In: Peter Loizos, Evthymios Papataxiarchis (eds.) *Contested Identities. Gender and Kinship in Modern Greece.* Princeton, N.J.: 221-234.

**Davis, John** (1977) *People of the Mediterranean: an Essay in Comparative Social Anthropology.* London.

**Deltsou, Eleftheria** (2000) '"Tourists", "Russian-Pontics", and "Native Greeks": Identity Politics in a Village in Northern Greece'. *Anthropological Journal on European Cultures*, 2000, 9/2: 31-51.

**Droukas, Eugenia** (1998) 'Albanians in the Greek informal economy'. *Journal of Ethnic and Migration Studies*, 24 (2): 347-365.

**Enepekidis, Polychronis** (1982) *Thessaloniki kai Makedonia 1798-1912 (Thessaloniki and Macedonia 1798-1912).* Athens.

**Enepekidis, Polychronis** (1988) *I Thessaloniki sta chronia 1875-1912 (Thessaloniki in the years 1875-1912).* Thessaloniki.

**Englert, Annette** (1995) *„Die Liebe kommt mit der Zeit". Interkulturelles Zusammenleben am Beispiel deutsch-ghanaischer Ehen in der BRD.* Münster.

**Europa auf einen Blick** 2007: ‚Griechenland': http://www.europa-auf-einen-blick.de/griechenland/wirtschaft.php [August 16 2007].

**European Commission** (2004) *The social situation in the European Union 2004.* EUROSTAT 2007: ‚European social statistics. Social protection - Expenditure and receipts. Data 1996-2004': http://www.uni-mannheim.de/edz/pdf/eurostat/07/KS-DC-07-001-EN.pdf [August 11 2007].

**Fakiolas, Rossetos.** (2000) 'Migration and Unregistered Labour in the Greek Economy', In: Russell King, Gabriella Lazaridis, Charalambos Tsardanidis (eds.), *Eldorado or Fortress? Migration in Southern Europe.* New York: 57-78.

**FEANTSA 2007**: http://www.feantsa.org/code/EN/pg.asp?Page=484 [February 23 2007]. Foundation for the Advancement of Sephardic Studies and Culture 2007: ‚Jewish Community of Thessaloniki (Salonika)': http://www.sephardicstudies.org/thes2.html [August 18 2007].

**Friedl, Ernestine** (1962) *Vasilika. A Village in Modern Greece.* New York.

**Gashi, Dardan; Steiner, Ingrid** (1997) *Albanien – Archaisch, Orientalisch, Europäisch.* Wien.

**General Secretariat Of National Statistical Service Of Greece** 2004: ‚Foreign Population by citizenship and sex': http://www.statistics.gr/eng_tables/S200_SPO_2_TB_AN_04_1_Y_EN.pdf [July 12 2006].

**Glasser, Irene; Bridgman, Rae** (1999) *Braving the Street. The Anthropology of Homelessness.* Oxford.

**Glick Schiller, Nina; Basch, Linda; Blanc-Szanton, Cristina.** (1992) 'Towards a definition of transnationalism: introductory remarks and research question'. In: N. Glick-Schiller, L. Basch, C. Blanc-Szanton (eds.) *Towards a Transnational Perspective on Migration: Race, Class, Ethnicity and Nationalism Reconsidered.* New York: ix-xiii.

**Glick Schiller, Nina; Basch, Linda; Blanc-Szanton, Cristina.** (1992) 'Transnationalism: a new analytic framework for understanding migration'. In: N. Glick-Schiller, L. Basch, C. Blanc-Szanton (eds.) *Towards a Transnational Perspective on Migration: Race, Class, Ethnicity and Nationalism Reconsidered.* New York: 1-24.

**Gjonça, Arjan** (2002) 'Albanische Emigration in den neunziger Jahren – eine neue Ära in der demographischen Entwicklung'. In: Karl Kaser, Robert Pichler, Stephanie Schwandner-Sievers (eds.) *Die weite Welt und das Dorf,* Wien, Köln, Weimar: 15-38.

**Goddard, Victoria** (1996) 'Food, Family and Community Memory'. In: V. Goddard, *Gender, Family and Work in Naples.* London: 205-232.

**Greiner, Clemens** (2003) *Der urbane Straßenhandel: eine wirtschaftsethnologische Analyse.* Wissenschaftliche Hausarbeit zur Erlangung des akademischen Grades eines Magister Artium der Universität Hamburg. Hamburg: unpubl. MA Thesis.

**Gruber, Martin** (2005) *Platzverweis: ethnologische Langzeituntersuchung einer Gruppe von Obdachlosen in der Hamburger Innenstadt.* Hamburg: unpubl. MA Thesis.

**Gust, Wolfgang** (1991) *Der Völkermord an den Armeniern. Die Tragödie des ältesten Christenvolkes der Welt.* München, Wien.

**Gutenschwager, Mary C.** (1971) *Nea Aeolia: Persistence and tradition in an urban Greek community.* Ann Arbor: Univ. of North Carolina at Chapel Hill.

**Haas, Elke** (2007) *Die albanische Migration als Diaspora? Eine vergleichende Untersuchung.* Hamburg: unpubl. MA Thesis

**Hadjitaki-Kapsomenou, Chrysoula** (2001) 'Folklore as Compensation: The Role of Local Cultural Associations in the Folklorisation of Social Memory in the Contemporary Greek Context'. In: *"Migration, Minorities, Compensation – Issues on cultural identity in Europe": papers presented on conference in Siena 2001.* (http://www.abo.fi/fak/hf/folklore/projekt/migration/Compensation.pdf); [February 22 2004].

**Haferkamp, Rose** (1989) *Afrikaner in der Fremde. Lehrjahre zwischen Wunsch und Wirklichkeit.* München.

**Halkos, George ; Salamouris, Dimitrios** (2003) 'Socio-economic integration of ethnic Greeks from the former USSR: obstacles to entry into the Greek labour market'. *Journal of Ethnic and Migration Studies* 29 (3): 519-534.

**Hamid, Ishraga Mustapha** (2003) ‚Die Situation afrikanischer Frauen in Wien'. In: Ebermann, Erwin (ed.): *Afrikaner in Wien. Zwischen Mystifizierung und Verteufelung. Erfahrungen und Analysen.* Münster: 26-31.

**Hatziprokopiou, Panos** (2003) 'Albanian immigrants in Thessaloniki, Greece: processes of economic and social incorporation'. *Journal of Ethnic Migration Studies*, 29 (6): 1033-1057.

**Hering, Gunnar; Demetriou, Georg; Kelpanides, Michael** (1980) ‚Politisches System'. In: Klaus-Detlev Grothusen (ed.): *Südosteuropa-Handbuch III: Griechenland.* Göttingen: 54-121.

**Herzfeld, Michael** (1982) *Ours once more. Folklore, Ideology and the Making of Modern Greece.* Austin.

**Herzfeld, Michael** (1991) *A Place in History. Social and Monumental Time in a Cretan Town.* Princeton, N.J.

**Hildebrand, Roman Ivanovic** (2005) *Georgische Küche. 612 Rezepte ausgewählt und bearbeitet von Roman I. Hildebrandt.* Wentorf bei Hamburg.

**Hirschon, Renée** (1989) *Heirs of the Greek catastrophe: The Social Life of Asia Minor Refugees in Piraeus.* Oxford.

**Hirschon, Renée** (ed.) (2003) *Crossing the Aegean : an appraisal of the 1923 compulsory population exchange between Greece and Turkey.* Studies in Forced Migration, Vol. 12. New York, Oxford.

**Ioannou, Iorgos** (1984) *I protevoussa to prosfygon (The capital of refugees).* Athens.

**Jähnig, Friederike; Vossenbrecker, Edith** (1990) ‚`Nächstes Jahr in der Heimat'. Probleme der Partisanenkinder bei der Rückkehr nach Griechenland'. In: Kokot, Waltraud (ed.): *Stadtmosaik. Beiträge zur ethnologischen Stadtforschung aus einer Feldexkursion nach Thessaloniki.* Bonn: 68-80.

**Jewish Community of Thessaloniki** 1996: ,The Jewish Community Of Thessaloniki Today': http://www.hri.org/culture97/eng/eidika_programmata/koinothtes/jewish_community/#AA3 [July 27 2005].

**Jewish Museum of Thessaloniki** 2005: http://www.jmth.gr/web/about.htm [July 19 2005].

**Jewish Museum of Thessaloniki** 2007: http://www.jmth.gr/web/thejews.htm [February 23 2007].

***Journal of Refugee Studies*** (1991), 4/4: Special Issue: The Odyssey of the Pontic Greeks.

**Karakatsanis, Neovi M.; Swarts, Jonathan** (2003) 'Migrant Women, Domestic Work and the Sex Trade in Greece – a Snapshot of Migrant Policy in the Making'. *The Greek Review of Social Research,* 110: 239-270.

**Karamanolis, Alkyone** (2006) *Grenzenlose Heimat. Die Migration nach Griechenland*: http://www.dradio.de/dlf/sendungen/hintergrundpolitik/460519 [January 27 2006].

**Karpozilos, Apostolos** (1991) 'Pontic Culture in the USSR between the Wars'. *Journal of Refugee Studies* 4/4, 1991: 364-371.

**Kaser, Karl** (2000) 'The history of the family in Albania in the 20th century: a first profile'. *Ethnologia Balkanica*, 4: 45-57.

**Kaser, Karl; Pichler, Robert; Schwandner-Sievers, Stephanie** (2002) 'Einleitung'. In: K. Kaser, R. Pichler, S. Schwandner-Sievers (eds.) *Die weite Welt und das Dorf,* Wien, Köln, Weimar: 7-13.

**Kelly, Ellen** (2005) 'Lifestyles and integration of Albanian women in Bologna'. In Russell King, Nicola Mai, Stephanie Schwandner-Sievers (eds.) *The New Albanian Migration*. Brighton and Portland: 29-63.

**Kenna, Margaret** (1977) 'Greek Urban Migrants and their rural patron saints'. *Ethnic Studies* 1: 14-23.

**Kennedy, Robinette** 1986: 'Women's Friendship on Crete: A Psychological Perspective'. In: Jill Dubisch (ed.) *Gender and Power in Rural Greece.* Princeton, N.J.: 121-138.

**Kiprianos, Pandelis; Balias, Stathis; Passas, Vaggelis** (2003) 'Greeks Policy towards Immigration and Immigrants'. *Social Policy and Administration.* 23/2: 148-164.

**Kirtsoglou, Elisabeth** (2004) *For the Love of Women. Gender, identity and same-sex relations in a Greek provincial town.* London, New York.

**Kitrilakis, Sotiris; Kitrilakis, Lidia** (2001): 'The Diet of the Greeks: 'Genetic' and Recent Memories'. In: Harlan Walker (ed.) *Food and the memory. Proceedings of the Oxford Symposium on Food and Cookery 2000.* Totnes: 131-135.

**Kokkinos, Dimitris** (1991a) 'The Greek State's Overview of the Pontian Issue'. *Journal of Refugee Studies* 4/4, 1991: 312-314.

**Kokkinos, Dimitris** (1991b) 'The Perception of Pontians from the Soviet Union in Greece'. *Journal of Refugee Studies* 4/4, 1991: 395-399.

**Kokot, Waltraud** (1995) *Kognition und soziale Identität in einem Flüchtlingsviertel: Kato Toumba, Thessaloniki*, Köln: unpubl. Habilitation Thesis

**Kokot, Waltraud** (1996) ‚Kleinasienflüchtlinge in Thessaloniki: zur Verarbeitung von Fluchterlebnissen in biographischen Erzählungen'. In: W. Kokot, Dorle Drackłé (eds.) *Ethnologie Europas: Grenzen, Konflikte, Identitäten.* Berlin: 259-272.

**Kokot, Waltraud** (2004) 'Diaspora – transnationale Beziehungen und Identitäten. Themen der Forschung in einem transnationalen Feld'. In: Christoph Marx (ed.) *Periplus. Jahrbuch für Aussereuropäische Geschichte 2004.* Münster, Hamburg, London: 1-10.

**Kokot, Waltraud** (2005) *European port cities: disadvantaged urban areas in transition: a collaborative project under the EU Transnational Exchange Programme ("Fight against Poverty and Social Exclusion"); Interim report - phase II / year 1.* Hamburg.

**Kokot, Waltraud; Lang, Hartmut** (2004) ‚Zur Konzeption des Lehrveranstaltungszyklus „Methoden der Ethnographie" im Lehrprogramm des Instituts für Ethnologie an der Universität Hamburg'. *Ethnoscripts.* 6/2. Hamburg: 103-108.

**Kokot, Waltraud; Tölölyan, Kachig; Alfonso, Carolin** (2004) 'Introduction'. In: W. Kokot, K. Tölölyan, C. Alfonso (eds.) *Diaspora, Identity and Religion. New Directions in Theory and Research.* London, New York: 1-8.

**Kokot, Waltraud; Wonneberger, Astrid** (2006) 'Editorial: Urbane Subsistenz'. *Ethnoscripts* 8/1, 2006: 2-6.

**Kokot, Waltraud (ed.)** (1990) *Stadtmosaik. Beiträge zur ethnologischen Stadtforschung aus einer Feldexkursion nach Thessaloniki.* Bonn.

**Koller, Hans Christoph** (2003) ‚Geschlechterrollen im Umbruch? Zur Bedeutung der Kategorie Geschlecht in biographischen Bildungsprozessen afrikanischer Migrant/innen in Deutschland am Beispiel von Studierenden aus Kamerun'. In: Verena Böll et al. (eds.): *Umbruch - Bewältigung - Geschlecht: Genderstudien zu afrikanischen Gesellschaften in Afrika und Deutschland.* Münster: 59-79.

**Kozlov, Victor** (1988) *The Peoples of the Soviet Union.* London.

**Kravva, Vasiliki** (2001) 'Food as a Vehicle for Remembering: the Case of the Thessalonikan Jews'. In: Harlan Walker (ed.) *Food and the memory. Proceedings of the Oxford Symposium on Food and Cookery 2000.* Totnes: 136-144.

**Kressing, Frank** (2002) 'General remarks on Albania and the Albanians'. In Frank Kressing, Karl Kaser (eds.) *Albania – a Country in Transition. Aspects of Changing Identities in a South-East European Country.* Baden-Baden: 11-25.

**Kyriakidou-Nestoros, Alki** (1978) *I theoria tis ellinikis laografias (The Theory of Greek Folklore).* Athens.

**Kyrtsis, Alexandros et al.** (2000) *Thessaloniki Odigos Polis (Thessaloniki City Guide).* Maroussi.

**Labrianidis, Lois; Hatziprokopiou, Panos** (2005) 'The Albanian migration cycle: Migrants tend to return to their country of origin after all'. In: Russell King, Nicola Mai, Stephanie Schwandner-Sievers (eds.) *The New Albanian Migration*, Brighton, Portland: 93-117.

**Labrianidis, Lois; Lyberaki, Antigone; Tinios, Platon; Hatziprokopiou, Panos** (2004) 'Inflow of Migrants and Outflow of Investment: Aspects of interdependence between Greece the Balkans'. *Journal of Ethnic and Migration Studies*, 30 (6): 1183-1208.

**Lang, Hartmut** (2002) ‚Vorbemerkungen zum Lehrveranstaltungszyklus "Methoden der Ethnographie" am Hamburger Institut für Ethnologie'. *Ethnoscripts* 4/1: 162-165.

**Lauth Bacas, Jutta** (2002) 'Greece and its New Immigrants: Features and Consequences the Recent Immigration to Greece'. *Ethnologia Balkanica*, 6: 197-207.

**Lazaridis, Gabriella** (2000) 'Filipino and Albanian Women Migrant Workers in Greece: Multiple Layers of Oppression'. In: Floya Anthias, Gabriella Lazaridis (eds.) *Gender and Migration in Southern Europe: Women on the Move.* Oxford and New York: 49-80.

**Lazaridis, Gabriella** (2001) 'Trafficking and Prostitution. The growing exploitation of Migrant Women in Greece'. *The European Journal of Women's Studies,* 2/2001; vol. 8: 67-102.

**Lazaridis, Gabriella; Psimmenos, Iordanis** (2000) 'Migrant Flows from Albania to Greece: Economic, Social and Spatial Exclusion'. In: Russell King, Gabriella Lazaridis, Charalambos Tsardanidis (eds.) *Eldorado or Fortress? Migration in Southern Europe.* New York: 170-185.

**Leven, Kathrin** (2006) *Migrationsziele – verwirklicht mit Hilfe von Diasporastrukturen? Eine Untersuchung am Beispiel afrikanischer Migrantinnen in Thessaloniki und Hamburg.* Hamburg: unpubl. MA Thesis.

**Levitt, Peggy** (2001) *The Transnational Villagers.* Berkley, Los Angeles, London.

**Lewkowicz, Beate** (1990a) *The Jewish community of Thessaloniki: a contemporary study.* Cambridge: unpubl. M. Phil. Thesis.

**Lewkowicz, Beate** (1990b) '"Griechenland ist meine Heimat, aber..." Das Selbstverständnis junger Juden in Thessaloniki'. In: Waltraud Kokot (ed.) *Stadtmosaik. Beiträge zur ethnologischen Stadtforschung aus einer Feldexkursion nach Thessaloniki.* Bonn: 80-96.

**Lewkowicz, Beate** (1994) '"Greece is my home, but...." Ethnic Identity of Greek Jews in Thessaloniki'. *Journal of Mediterranean Studies* 4, 2: 225-247.

**Lewkowicz, Beate** (2006) *The Jewish community of Salonika: history, memory, identity.* London, Portland, OR.

**Loizos, Peter; Papataxiarchis, Evthymios** (1991) 'Gender and Kinship in Marriage and Alternative Contexts'. In: P. Loizos, E. Papataxiarchis (eds.): *Contested Identities. Gender and Kinship in Modern Greece.* Princeton, N.J.: 3-25.

**Loizos, Peter, E. Papataxiarchis** (eds.) (1991) *Contested Identities. Gender and Kinship in Modern Greece.* New York.

**Mai, Nicola** (2002) 'Jugend und italienische Medien'. In: Karl Kaser, Robert Pichler, Stephanie Schwandner-Sievers (eds.) *Die weite Welt und das Dorf.* Wien, Köln, Weimar: 39-62.

**Mai, Nicola** (2005) 'The Albanian Diaspora-in-the-Making'. *Journal of Ethnic and Migration Studies*, 31 (3): 543-561.

**Mai, Nicola; Schwandner-Sievers, Stephanie** (2003) 'Albanian Migration and New Transnationalism'. *Journal of Ethnic and Migration Studies*, 29 (6): 939-948.

**Maratou-Alipranti, Laura; Fakiolas, Rossetos** (2003) 'The Lonely Path of Migrant Women in Greece'. *The Greek Review of Social Research, 110*: 165-188.

**Mark, Rudolf A.** (1989) *Die Völker der Sowjetunion: ein Lexikon.* Opladen.

**Martin, Claude** (1997) ‚Social Welfare and the Familiy in Southern Europe'. In: Martin Rhodes (ed.): *Southern European Welfare States. Between Crisis and Reform.* London, Portland OR: 23-41.

**Mavromatis, Miltos** (1996) *"Ladadika". Apo tin enkatalipsi stin diasosi. To egchirima mias allis politikis tis diachirisis (Ladadika - from dereliction to rescue).* Thessaloniki.

**Mazower, Mark** (2004) *Salonica: City of Ghosts. Christians Muslims and Jews 1430 - 1950.* London.

**McIntyre, Joseph** (2004) ‚Die Migration aus Afrika nach Deutschland'. In: J. McIntyre, Beate Balliel, Katrin Pfeiffer (eds.) *Wurzeln in zwei Welten. Westafrikanische Migrantinnen und Migranten in Hamburg.* Frankfurt a.M: 27-36.

**Mennell, Stephen; Murcott, Anne; Otterloo, Anneke H. van** (1992) *The Sociology of Food: Eating, Diet and Culture.* London, Newbury Park, New Delhi.

**Meyer, Dorothea** (1994) ‚„Geschminkt und gut gewaschen": Frauenbilder und weibliche Prostitution in Griechenland'. In: Uta Holter (ed.): *Bezahlt, geliebt, verstoßen. Prostitution und andere Sonderformen institutionalisierter Sexualität in verschiedenen Kulturen.* Bonn: 69-84.

**Middelton, Sue; Barnes, Matt; Millar, Jane** (2003) 'Introduction: the dynamic analysis of poverty and social exclusion'. In: Eleni Apospori, Jane Millar (eds.): *The Dynamics of Social Exclusion in Europe. Comparing Austria, Germany, Greece, Portugal and the UK.* Cheltenham: 1-15.

**Molho, Anthony** (1991) 'The Jewish Community of Salonika: The End of a Long History'.- *Diaspora* 1(1): 100-122.

**Molho, Michael** (ed.) (1981) *In Memoriam. Gewidmet dem Andenken an die jüdischen Opfer der Naziherrschaft in Griechenland.* Essen.

**Molho, Rena** (1988) `The Jewish Community of Salonica and its Incorporation into the Greek State , 1912-19´. *Middle Eastern Studies*. 24: 391-403.

**Molho, Rena** (2001) *Oi Evreai tis Thessalonikis, 1856-1919: Mia Idiaiteri Koinotita* (The Jews of Thessaloniki 1956-1919, a special community). Athens.

**Momeni, Jamshid A.** (1990) 'No Place to Go: A National Picture of Homelessness in America'. In: Jamshid A. Momeni, Gerald R. Garrett (eds.) *Homelessness in the United States. Volume II: Data and Issues,* New York: 165-183.

**Moutzopoulos, Nikos** (1980) *Thesssaloniki 1900-1917.* Thessaloniki.

**Neuber, Harald** (2005) ‚Tatkraft und Tradition'. *Jüdische Allgemeine (November 10 2005):* (http://www.widerstand-repression-griechenland.de/hinter/div/juedischeAllgemeine-2005-11-10.html) [August 18 2007].

**Newspaper of Athens** 2006: '*Interview with Albert Spiegel and David Saltiel*': Homepage of the German State Department: Holocaust-Gedenktag in Thessaloniki mit Bundesminister Joschka Fischer: Gemeinsames Interview von Botschafter Dr. Albert Spiegel und dem Vorsitzenden der jüdischen Gemeinde Thessaloniki, David Saltiel in der Athener Zeitung: http://www.athen.diplo.de/Vertretung/athen/de/02/Archiv/Holocaust__Gedenktag__in__Thessaloniki__mit__Bundesminister__Joschka__Fischer.html [July 28 2007].

**Novac, Sylvia; Brown, Joyce; Gallant, Gloria** (1999) *Women on the rough edge : a decade of change for long-term homeless women,* Ottawa.

**Nsodu, Mbinglo** (2004) *Black Angels in the White Man's Country,* Ghana.

**Pack, Monika** (1991) *Ethnische Identität bei pontischen Griechen in Köln,* Köln: unpubl. MA thesis.

**Papadopoulou-Symeonidou, Parystatis** (1975) *Boden- und gebäudewirtschaftliche Probleme der Stadtplanung am Beispiel Thessalonikis.* Berlin.

**Papagiannopoulos, Apostolos** (1982) *Istoria tis Thessalonikis. (History of Thessaloniki).* Thessaloniki.

**Papajoannou, Maria; Traganou, Olga** (1974) *Meleti tis dimiourgias ton astikon profygikon oikismon kai paratiriseis jia tin symerini tous katastasi (The Developement and Contemporary Situation of Urban Refugee Quaters).* Thessaloniki: unpubl. Diploma Thesis.

**Papataxiarchis, Evthymios** (1991) 'Friends of the Heart: Male Commensal Solidarity, Gender and Kinship in Aegean Greece'. In: Peter Loizos, Evthymios Papataxiarchis (eds.) *Contested Identities. Gender and Kinship in Modern Greece.* Princeton, N.J.: 156-179.

**Passaro, Joanne** (1996) *The Unequal Homeless: Men on the Streets, Women in Their Place.* London, New York.

**Peters, Richard** (1961) *Geschichte der Türken.* Stuttgart.

**Phizacklea, Annie** (2000) 'The politics of belonging, sex work, domestic work: transnational household strategies'. In: Sallie Westwood, A. Phizacklea (eds.) *Transnationalism and the Politics of Belonging.* London, New York: 120-145.

**Phizacklea, Annie** (2003) 'Transnationalism, gender and global workers'. In: Mirjana Morokvasic-Müller, Umut Erel, Kyoko Shinozaki (eds.) *Crossing Borders and Shifting Boundaries.* Opladen: 79-100.

**Pichler, Robert** (2002) ,Hirten, Söldner und Wnaderarbeiter. Formen der mobilen Ökonomie in den Dörfern des südalbanischen Hochlandes'. In: Karl Kaser, Robert Picher, Stephanie Schwandner-Sievers (eds.) *Die weite Welt und das Dorf.* Wien, Köln: 133-161.

**Piperno, Flavia** (2005) 'Albanian migrants' remittances: A development opportunity?'. In: Russell King, Nicola Mai, Stephanie Schwandner-Sievers (eds.) *The New Albanian Migration.* Brighton and Portland: 118-138.

**PONS** (2000) *Kompaktwörterbuch für alle Fälle: Neugriechisch – Deutsch.* 1. neubearb. Aufl. – Nachdruck 2002, bearb. von: Dimitrios Karagiannnakis et al. unter Mitwirkung und Leitung der Redaktion PONS Wörterbücher. Stuttgart.

**Prohazka, Martin** (2002) 'Das Dorf, Albanien und die Welt'. In: Karl Kaser, Robert Pichler, Stephanie Schwandner-Sievers (eds.) *Die weite Welt und das Dorf.* Wien, Köln, Weimar: 239-261.

**Psarrou, Nelly** (2004) 'The Greek diaspora in Eastern Europe and the Former Soviet Union'. In: Jochen Blaschke (ed.): *Migration and Political Intervention. Diasporas in Transition Countries.* Berlin.

**Psimenos, Iordanis** (2000) 'The Making of Periphractic Spaces: The Case of Albanian Undocumented Female Migrants in the Sex Industry of Athens'. In: Floya Anthias, Gabriella Lazaridis (eds.): *Gender and Migration Southern Europe. Women on the Move.* Oxford, New York: 81-101.

**Rapti, Ourania** (2006) 'The dockworkers of Thessaloniki: Past and Present.'. *Ethnoscripts 8/1.*: 22-35.

**Rhodes, Martin** (1997) 'Southern European Welfare States: Identity, Problems and Prospects for Reform'. In: M. Rhodes (ed.) *Southern European Welfare States. Between Crisis and Reform.* London: 1-22

**Richter, Heinz A.** (1973) *Griechenland zwischen Revolution und Konterrevolution 1936-1946.* Frankfurt/M.

**Richter, Heinz A.** (1988) ‚Aspekte der griechischen Zeitgeschichte'. *Das Parlament, Beilage 14-15, 1988*: 25-35.

**Richter, Heinz A.** (1990) *Griechenland im 20. Jahrhundert. Band 1: Megali Idea - Republik - Diktatur.* Köln.

**Rothschild, Walter** (2002) *99 Fragen zum Judentum.* Gütersloh.

**Safran, William** (1999) 'Comparing diasporas: A review essay'. *Diaspora* 8 (3): 255-291.

**Sapounakis, Aristide** (2003) *National Review of Policies, Research and Statistics on Access to Housing and Homelessness.* Athens: European Observatory on Homelessness (FEANTSA)

**Sapounakis, Aristide** (2004) *Greece National Report 2004 for the European Observatory on Homelessness: Statistical Update.* Athens: European Observatory on Homelessness (FEANTSA)

**Schöttes, Martina; Treibel, Anette** (1997) ‚Frauen - Flucht - Migration . Wanderungsmotive von Frauen und Aufnahmesituation in Deutschland'. In: Ludger Pries (ed.) *Transnationale Migration.* Baden-Baden: 85-117.

**Schwalgin, Susanne** (1995) *Die Stoa Modiano : Ethnographie und Geschichte eines Marktes in Thessaloniki.* Bonn.

**Schwalgin, Susanne** (2004) *„Wir werden niemals vergessen!": Trauma, Erinnerung und Identität in der armenischen Diaspora Griechenlands.* Bielefeld.

**Semmler, Ruth** (1990): ‚„Meine Eltern haben immer Griechenland als Paradies gesehen ...": Orientierungsprobleme junger Remigrantinnen aus der Bundesrepublik'. In: Waltraud Kokot (ed.): *Stadtmosaik. Beiträge zur ethnologischen Stadtforschung aus einer Feldexkursion nach Thessaloniki.* Bonn: 53-67.

**Shlay, Anne B.; Rossi, Peter H.** (1992) 'Social Science Research and Contemporary Studies of Homelessness'. *Annual Review of Sociology*: 129-160.

**Spengler-Axiopoulos, Barbara** (1992) *Die jüdische Präsenz in Thessaloniki. Gestern und Heute.* Göttingen: unpub. MA Thesis

**Spengler-Axiopoulos, Barbara** (1998) '*Das kleine Jerusalem an der Ägäis - eine Erinnerung an das jüdische Saloniki*'. Griechische Gemeinde Göttingen: http://www.giannaris.net/Teyxos5/Sprengler-Axiopoulou.Salonikh.htm [February 1 2002].

**Spengler-Axiopoulos, Barbara** (2001) ‚Grosse Mutter der Armen. Griechenland zwischen Multikulturalität und Ethnozentrismus', *Neue Zürcher Zeitung* - Literatur und Kunst, Oct. 6 2001, 232/82; (http://www.kzu.ch/fach/as/aktuell/2001/09_griechenland/11_02_bm.htm) [February 27 2004].

**Stathakis, Pamela** (2002a) ‚Der pontisch griechische Exodus I – Die Einwanderung von Griechen aus der ehemaligen UdSSR nach Griechenland'. *neaFon* 1/2002: 52-58.

**Stathakis, Pamela** (2002b) ‚Der pontisch griechische Exodus II – Die Einwanderung von Griechen aus der ehemaligen UdSSR nach Griechenland'. *neaFon* 2/2002: 76-85.

**Statistisches Bundesamt** (2007) *Löhne und Gehälter. Verdienste, Arbeitskosten und Arbeitszeiten im Ausland – Vergleichende Übersichten (Ausgabe 2006).* Wiesbaden.

**Straub, Eberhard** (2000) ‚Ladino'. In: Julius H. Schoeps (ed.): *Neues Lexikon des Judentums*, Gütersloh: 465.

**Stroux, Salinia** (2006) 'Afghan, Iranian and Iraqi Street Vendors in Thessaloniki, Greece: Street Vending as Survival Entrepreneurship'. *Ethnoscripts 8/1*: 36-61.

**Sutton, David E.** (2001) *Remembrance of Repasts: An Anthropology of Food and Memory.* Oxford, New York.

**Symeonidou, Haris** 1997: 'Social Protection in Contemporary Greece'. In: Martin Rhodes (ed.) *Southern European Welfare States. Between Crisis and Reform.* London: 67-86.

**Tastsoglou, Evangelia; Hadjicostandi, Joanna** (2003) 'Never Outside the Labour Market, but always Outsiders: Female migrant workers in Greece'. *The Greek Review of Social Research*, 110: 189-220.

**Thessaloniki Port Authority** 2007: http://www.thpa.gr/en/thessaloniki/thessaloniki_short.htm [June 2007].

**Triandafyllidou, Anna; Veikou, Mariangela** (2002) 'The hierarchy of Greekness: Ethnic and national identity considerations in Greek immigration policy'. *Ethnicities* 2(2): 189-208.

**Tsakloglou, Panos** (2003) 'The risk of multidimensional disadvantage and social exclusion during for life stages in a dynamic perspective'. In: Eleni Apospori, Jane Millar (eds.) *The Dynamics of Social Exclusion in Europe. Comparing Austria, Germany, Greece, Portugal and the UK.* Cheltenham: 16-40.

**Underwood, Jackson** (1993) *The bridge people: daily life in a camp of the homeless.* Lanham.

**UNDP** (2000) Albanian Human Development Report. Tirana.

**Vakalopoulos, Apostolos** (1983) Istoria *tis Thessalonikis (History of Thessaloniki).* Thessaloniki.

**Vakalopoulos, Apostolos** (1985) *Griechische Geschichte von 1204 bis heute.* Köln.

**Van den Berghe, Pierre** (1984) 'Ethnic cuisine, culture in nature'. *Ethnic and Racial Studies*: 7(3): 387-97.

**Vergeti, Maria** (1991) 'Pontic Greeks from Asia Minor and the Soviet Union: Problems of Integration in Modern Greece'. *Journal of Refugee Studies* 4/4, 1991: 382-394.

**Vermeulen, Cornelis Jacob Johannes** (1970) *Families in Urban Greece.* Cornell.

**Voutira, Eftihia** (1991) 'Pontic Greeks Today: Migrants or Refugees?´. *Journal of Refugee Studies* 4/4, 1991: 400-420.

**Voutira, Eftihia** (1997a) 'Population Transfer and Resettlement Policies in Inter-War Europe: The Case of Asia Minor Refugees in Macedonia from an International and National Perspective'. In: Peter Mackridge, Eleni Yannakakis (eds.): *The Development of a Greek Macedonian Cultural Identity Since 1912,* Oxford, New York: 111-131.

**Voutira, Eftihia** (1997b) 'Dilemmas of identity and national belonging among the Greek diaspora in the former Soviet Union'. Paper presented at the Seminar Series organised by the Greek General Consulate and the Institute of Social and Cultural Anthropology. Hamburg, 22/11/1997.

**Voutira, Eftihia** (2003a) 'When Greeks meet other Greeks: Settlement Policy Issues in the Contemporary Greek Context'. In: Renée Hirschon, (ed.): *Crossing the Aegean : an appraisal of the 1923 compulsory population exchange between Greece and Turkey.* New York, Oxford: 145-159.

**Voutira, Eftihia** (2003b) 'Refugees: whose term is it anyway? *Emic* and *etic* constructions of 'refugees' in Modern Greek'. In: Joanne van Selm et al. (eds.): *The Refugee Convention at fifty: a view from forced migration studies*: 65-80.

**Voutira, Eftihia** (2004) „Metanastevsi stin patrida". *Meionotites stin Ellada, Epistimoniko Symposio me Thema Meionotites stin Ellada (7 - 9 Noemvriou 2002), Etaireia Spoudon Neoellinikou Politismou kai Genikis Paideias.* („Immigration to the Motherland", in: *Minorities in Greece, Association for Studies of Modern Greek Culture and General Education.* Athens: 233-259.

**Walker, Christopher J.** (ed.) (1991) *Armenia and Karabagh. The struggle for unity.* London.

**Westwood, Sallie; Phizacklea, Annie** (2000) 'Introduction'. In S. Westwood, A. Phizacklea (eds.) *Trans-nationalism and the Politics of Belonging.* London: 1-16.

**Wiebe, Dietrich** (1978) ‚Marktzyklen und Marktformen in Thessaloniki/Griechenland'. *Zeitschrift für Wirtschaftsgeographie, Angewandte und Sozialgeographie*: 22/8: 239-245.

**Wolch, Jennifer R.; Dear, Michael** (1993) *Malign neglect : homelessness in an American city.* San Francisco.

**Xanthopoulou-Kyriakou, Artemis** (1991) ‚The Diaspora of the Greeks of the Pontos'. *Journal of Refugee Studies* 4/4, 1991: 357-363.

**lines**
Beiträge zur Stadtforschung aus dem Institut für Ethnologie der Universität Hamburg
hrsg. von Prof. Dr. Waltraud Kokot

Waltraud Kokot; Martin Gruber
**Betroffene von Räumungsklagen und Verbleib von Zwangsgeräumten**
Eine ethnologische Untersuchung zu Lebenssituation und Verbleibsalternativen
Täglich werden Hamburg mehrere Wohnungen zwangsweise geräumt. Arbeitslosigkeit, Armut und die damit verbundenen Probleme sind vordringliche Gründe für den Verlust der Wohnung, der in vielen Fällen in die Obdachlosigkeit führt. Wie verhalten sich Menschen in dieser Situation? Welche Gründe haben dazu geführt und welche Strategien stehen ihnen zur Verfügung, nachdem sie ihre Wohnung verloren haben? Der vorliegende Bericht ist das Ergebnis einer Feldforschung des Instituts für Ethnologie der Universität Hamburg von Dezember 2005 bis Juli 2006.
Bd. 3, Herbst 2007, ca. 80 S., ca. 9,90 €, br., ISBN 978-3-8258-0298-1

LIT Verlag Berlin – Hamburg – London – Münster – Wien – Zürich
Fresnostr. 2 48159 Münster
Tel.: 0251 / 620 32 22 – Fax: 0251 / 922 60 99
e-Mail: vertrieb@lit-verlag.de – http://www.lit-verlag.de

**lines**
Beiträge zur Stadtforschung aus dem Institut für Ethnologie der Universität Hamburg
hrsg. von Prof. Dr. Waltraud Kokot

Waltraud Kokot (Hg.)
**Kultur der Obdachlosigkeit in der Hamburger Innenstadt**
Eine ethnologische Felduntersuchung
Bd. 1, Herbst 2007, ca. 72 S., ca. 6,90 €, br., ISBN 978-3-8258-0048-2

Waltraud Kokot; Helmut Rösing; Simone Reich; Simon Sell (Hg.)
**„Die härteste Bühne der Welt ... ": Straßenmusik in Hamburg**
Ethnologische und musikwissenschaftliche Annäherungen. Mit einer CD
Bd. 2, Herbst 2007, ca. 72 S., ca. 5,90 €, br., ISBN 3-8258-0049-0

**Berliner Ethnographische Studien**
Kulturwissenschaftlich-ethnologische Untersuchungen zu Alltagsgeschichte, Alltagskultur und Alltagswelten in Europa
hrsg. vom Institut für Europäische Ethnologie der Humboldt-Universität zu Berlin

Thomas Kochan
**Den Blues haben**
Momente einer jugendlichen Subkultur in der DDR
Bd. 2, 2002, 112 S., 9,90 €, br., ISBN 3-8258-5998-3

Anja Schwanhäußer
**Stilrevolte Underground**
Die Alternativkultur als Agent der Postmoderne
Bd. 3, 2002, 104 S., 15,90 €, br., ISBN 3-8258-6171-6

Asta Vonderau
**Geographie sozialer Beziehungen**
Ortserfahrungen in der mobilen Welt
Bd. 4, 2003, 88 S., 9,90 €, br., ISBN 3-8258-6493-6

Johanna Keller
**Neue Nomaden?**
Zur Theorie und Realität aktueller Migrationsbewegungen in Berlin
Bd. 6, 2005, 96 S., 9,90 €, br., ISBN 3-8258-8287-x

Alexandra Schwell
**Anarchie ist die Mutter der Ordnung**
Alternativkultur und Tradition in Polen
Bd. 7, 2005, 144 S., 9,90 €, br., ISBN 3-8258-8393-0

Jens Adam
**„Kaum noch normale Berliner"**
Stadtethnologische Erkundungen in einem „sozialen Problemquartier"
Bd. 8, 2005, 136 S., 9,90 €, br., ISBN 3-8258-8451-1

Christine Nippe
**Kunst der Verbindung**
Transnationale Netzwerke, Kunst und Globalisierung
Bd. 9, 2006, 120 S., 9,90 €, br., ISBN 3-8258-9115-1

Ann-Kathrin Zöckler
**Unternehmerinnen des Wandels**
Erwerbsbiographien und -strategien andalusischer Existenzgründerinnen
Bd. 10, 2006, 120 S., 9,90 €, br., ISBN 3-8258-9365-0

Thomas Götz
**Stadt und Sound**
Das Beispiel Bristol
Seattle Grunge, Hamburger Schule, Manchester Sound. Trägt die Stadt dazu bei wie Musik klingt? Verweisen lokale Szenen und ihre Sounds auf die Charakteristiken einer Stadt? Diese Fragen rücken zusehends in den Blickwinkel der Kultur- und Sozialwissenschaften. Der vorliegende Band betrachtet die vielseitigen Wechselbeziehungen von Stadt und Musik am Beispiel des Bristol Sounds, den Interpreten wie Massive Attack, Smith and Mighty und Portishead repräsentieren. Der Autor beschreibt die Entstehung, den Höhepunkt und den Abstieg eines urbanen Sounds, der sich im Spannungsfeld globaler und lokaler Einflüsse bewegt. „Thomas Götz hat mit seiner Arbeit nicht nur einen wichtigen, neue inhaltliche Perspektiven zum Verhältnis von Stadt und Sound erschließenden Beitrag geleistet, sondern auch zu einer urban anthropology, die das Gebilde ‚Stadt' in seinen Fokus nimmt. Die Arbeit besticht vor allem durch methodische Vielfalt und argumentative Reflexivität; sie ist ein exemplarisches Beispiel für ein behutsames, dennoch entschiedenes Argumentieren im besten Sinne des Wortes." Rolf Lindner
Bd. 11, 2006, 112 S., 9,90 €, br., ISBN 3-8258-9700-1

LIT Verlag Berlin – Hamburg – London – Münster – Wien – Zürich
Fresnostr. 2 48159 Münster
Tel.: 0251 / 620 32 22 – Fax: 0251 / 922 60 99
e-Mail: vertrieb@lit-verlag.de – http://www.lit-verlag.de